NEIL MCKENTY
LIVE!

—The lines are still blazing—

Alan Hustak
with
Catharine McKenty

Torchflame Books
An imprint of Light Messages

Neil McKenty Live - The lines are still blazing
www.neilmckenty.com

Published in 2014 by Shoreline Press, Montreal
Published 2015, by Torchflame Books
    an Imprint of Light Messages
www.lightmessages.com
Durham, NC 27713 USA
ISBN: 978-1-61153-185-5

Cover design by Yannick Allen-Larochelle
Cover Photograph by John Mahoney
Cartoons by Aislin

Contents

For all those on the journey to wholeness

What would you do if you won $2 million dollars?

I'd buy CJAD and have Neil McKenty fired.

A few minutes later, another caller chortled,

I'd buy back the radio station from the previous caller and hire Neil McKenty back.

Sometimes people find my opinions upsetting. It is one of the hazards of my work. So people disagree with me, so what?
I expect that.

–Neil McKenty.

Neil and Catharine in the garden of The Priory on Pine Ave, 1980.

Introduction –
Enter Catharine

Neil McKenty swept me off my feet on a dance floor at an event sponsored by Hiatus, an Arts and Letters Club with a sense of humour. We had gone out on a date about six months earlier. That evening I had said to myself "This guy is impossible" and sent him packing. But I kept thinking about him, and when I saw a reference to his biography of Mitch Hepburn in the *Globe and Mail*, I phoned him. For ten nights after that we went out dining, dancing, to the theatre. Six weeks later on August 19, 1972, we were married.

At the time I was an Ontario government speechwriter. I had only recently come back to Toronto after 13 years in the United States, six of them as a researcher for Pace magazine in Los Angeles. Before that I had spent four years as a volunteer in the war-torn Ruhr mining area of Germany after earning a degree in English at the University of Toronto's Victoria College.

Neil was just finishing a three-year stint as Executive Director of the Harry E. Foster Charitable Foundation, the "first real paying job" he had ever had, advancing the cause of the intellectually handicapped. With the Foundation, he joined forces with the Kennedy family and Brian O'Neill of the National

Hockey League, to bring the Special Olympics to Canada. For the first time floor hockey was included in the games.

Now he was looking for a new challenge. An advertisement in the *Globe and Mail* for a "Director of Public Affairs" at a radio station in a large metropolitan city caught his eye. It turned out to be at CJAD in Montreal, which had a reputation as one of the best stations in the country. Neil got the job in a field of 60 candidates.

Two weeks after our honeymoon we moved lock, stock, and barrel into a small apartment behind the old Montreal Forum. Neil went on the air barely knowing where the corner of Peel and Ste. Catherine was. With little money and no car we explored this marvelous city. At four o'clock on a November afternoon, in the middle of a snowstorm, we relished our first smoked meat sandwich at Schwartz's. Soon after we discovered breakfast at Beautys on Mount Royal Ave., a split order of delectable blueberry pancakes and sausages, washed down with strong coffee. With each visit, Beautys owner and founder, Hymie Sckolnick welcomed us as if we were part of his extended family. "We are not here to make money, but to make you happy," he'd say. And indeed he did.

Life with Neil was a continuing adventure. I was married to an absolutely unique human being. I never knew which side of his complex, bipolar personality I would be dealing with on any given day. I once told him that, if he had not been a Jesuit for 26 years, he would have been a high-priced lawyer with three divorces behind him. I, on the other hand, came from a strict, close-knit Protestant family with roots in Northern Ireland. As Neil once said, our marriage should not have worked, but it did. I have talked with many people whose family lives have been affected by the ravages of bipolar disorder, as mine was. We've had the tragic death of the much-loved comic genius Robin Williams. My hope is that this book will help raise awareness, and bring both laughter and hope in difficult times.

It always seemed to me that radio liberated Neil's spirit in a special way and now his death has done that to an immeasurably greater degree.

It has been a delight for me to work on this project with a team from both sides of the Atlantic: Richard Rice who had archived a great deal of Neil's material, first had the idea of creating a scrapbook. I began by hauling out boxes and plastic bags and an old black suitcase full of material. Six drafts and 500 pages later my brain began to fry. My heartfelt thanks to veteran journalist Alan Hustak, who knew Neil as a priest and taught Alan at Campion College who then put his editorial skills to work and compiled the material for this edition. Thanks also to The *Gazette* for permission to reproduce a number of articles, especially Terry Mosher for the use of his cartoons. In putting this book together I have discovered aspects of Neil's life and career of which I was unaware, even though we had been married for 40 years.

I have been aided by Marion Blake, herself an astute editor and writer who gave me wise advice from day one. John McKenty, Neil's nephew, himself a published author, came on board as did Clare Hallward, who had helped edit several of Neil's books. My thanks also to Paul Belyea, John Fleming, Cynthia MacDonald, Barbara Moser and Thelma Geary at the Senior Times, Jean Plourde, Harold and Barbara Thuringer, and Stéphanie Pagano, our goddaughter.

Neil's long time friend and mentor, Jim Reed, invested hundreds of hours sorting through material and listening to tapes that were loaned by Holly Haimerl who worked with Neil at CJAD. To my great delight, Judy Isherwood who had turned Neil's memoir, *The Inside Story* into a best seller, agreed to publish this manuscript. To all of you who have contributed to this portrait of Neil, my thanks.

Catharine Fleming McKenty

A new edition of Catharine's own book *Polly of Bridgewater Farm* (Torchflame Books) is now available on Amazon.

Neil McKenty, S.J.

Foreword

He was Father Neil McKenty, S.J. when we first met in 1961 at Campion College, a Jesuit boarding school in Regina. I was a student there and Neil had come to preach a retreat. Neil loved to argue for the hell of it, even when he was a priest, and he made a career out of doing just that. By the time I ran into him in Montreal ten years or so later, he had left the Jesuits, married, and we were both working as journalists – Neil at CJAD, and me at the CBC. It took me awhile to shake the habit of calling him "Father McKenty." I didn't appreciate until much later that for the 26 years he spent in the priesthood he had been a conflicted cleric who couldn't reconcile what was going on in his own head with the hypocrisy of the moral absolutes taught by the Vatican. So he quit and went on to become the highest-rated radio talk show host in Montreal.

His show, "Exchange," became a sort of public confessional, a safe space where listeners could indeed exchange ideas in an atmosphere of civility. The message he preached on the air was one of human decency, not petty cant or dogma. At the peak of his career more than 75,000 people tuned in.

"The basic exchange on 'Exchange,' is not between the listeners and Neil McKenty," McKenty once explained why he thought the show was so successful, "It is between the listeners. If the host sets up the chemistry, the show goes on its own momentum and I am almost on the sidelines. On the other hand, I am in the entertainment business. If I bore my listeners, I'm dead."

Throughout most of his life Neil was afflicted with depression, a disorder of mood which the writer William Styron described as being "so painful and elusive that it becomes known to the self – to the mediating intellect – as to verge close to being beyond description." Neil, however, saw his depression as "a fundamental spiritual experience," which he chronicled in his revealing autobiography *The Inside Story.*

On the air, he was always in his element. He was never condescending, he didn't often antagonize, nor would he frame overly complex problems with simple sound bites. But often he ducked answering the very questions he asked, answering a question, in true Jesuit fashion, with a question, leaving it up to his listeners to argue the merits of the point he was wishing to make. Neil McKenty was born December 31, 1924, and grew up in Hastings, Ontario, where his father, Arthur, ran the local hardware store. His mother, Irene, was a school teacher. Arthur McKenty fought with the 57th Canadian Regiment and was wounded at Passchendaele. Although he was undoubtedly a courageous man, the war traumatized Neil's father. He drank heavily to forget and preached a hard religious line.

Neil was taught by Redemptorist priests, "religious terrorists," as he put it, who instilled the fear of God in him. He was also an altar boy who served Mass for the parish priest who, as he recalled, "took out his suffering on his parishioners."

Hastings was a Protestant town. Growing up as a Roman Catholic during the Depression, Neil felt isolated, and thought that he was an outsider. Shy and withdrawn, he first became aware of the power of radio in his teens listening to religious radio programs. He wrote his first essay on the Spanish Civil War and by the age of 15 he was "a stringer," for the *Peterborough Examiner.*

Neil and his younger brother were further educated by Jesuits at Regiopolis College in Kingston He took his B.A. at St. Michael's College in Toronto before entering the Society of Jesus as a novice in 1944. He was ordained in 1957, worked in New York as a relief editor for a summer with the Jesuit publication *America*, and spent time in London. He returned to study history at the University of Toronto; his doctoral thesis, and subsequent book, was a biography of Ontario premier Mitch Hepburn. He had worked for the Liberal Party in the 1943 provincial election campaign.

It was during a visit to Rome that he began to have misgivings about the institutional church, which he described as "a bloated structure, top heavy with oppressive authority." By 1969 he had made up his mind to leave the priesthood. "When it came to preaching, I had a lot going for me," he once said, but he was unable to reconcile the fact that what he was saying in his homilies "didn't jibe with my feelings about those words in my heart."

After leaving the Jesuits, he worked in Toronto for the Harry E. Foster Charitable Foundation for the intellectually disabled, and helped organize the first Special Olympics to be held in Quebec. In 1972 he was hired to do talk show radio in Montreal. While he was in his element behind the microphone, McKenty was rarely happy being a public figure. He bared his dark night of the soul in a no-holds barred autobiography, *The Inside Story*, in which, among other things, he revealed that he was a recovering alcoholic, never took his priestly vows of celibacy seriously, and had even thought of killing himself.

Although he left the priesthood he embraced a spiritual approach to spiritual discipline which was rooted in a papal encyclical, *Gaudium et Spes*. Neil believed there were no moral absolutes, that we all have a right to act in freedom with an informed conscience when it comes to making moral decisions. He believed in the Gospels as a manual to help guide what we do, but not how we do it. He kept a blog and wrote a regular column, "Pit Stop," for the *Senior Times*.

He continued to rail against the Vatican, and one wonders what he would make of the musings of Pope Francis, another Jesuit, who recently railed against rigid religious ideology. "When a Christian becomes a disciple of ideology, he has lost the faith and is no longer a disciple of Jesus; he is instead, a disciple of this rigid attitude of thinking," the Pope said. "For this reason, Jesus says to them, 'You have taken away the key of knowledge.' The faith becomes ideology, and ideology chases away the people, distances the people and distances the church from the people. It is a serious illness, this of ideological Christians. It is an illness, but it is not new, eh?"

Sounds like something Neil would have said. I wish he were alive to hear it.

The introductory paragraph in italics at the beginning of certain chapters is by Alan Hustak as narrator.

Alan Hustak
A.M.D.G.

1

Neil's Personal Creed

Although I left the Jesuit priesthood in 1969 I still consider myself a practicing Roman Catholic. Those of us who believe in a God and believe we have been created in the image of God, relate to God in our own way. Some do not relate to God at all. What I do believe is that God writes straight with crooked lines, that everyone has to experience a degree of personal suffering to become more whole. We develop ourselves from the inside out. Most people are not comfortable in their own skin and seek ways to relieve their discomfort, often trying to fill a spiritual vacuum with material things. That is why there is such a spiritual malaise in the Western world and why so many people, particularly younger people, are leaving traditional religion to experiment, especially with religions of the East.

I think we must lose our life in order to find it. What I had to lose was my obsessive need to control. This need was so pervasive, so embedded in my bones, that a spiritual crisis had to occur for me to fall to my knees and ask for help. Whatever it is, we must endure a painful experience that transforms the way we feel about ourselves and the way we perceive the world. It involves relying on a power greater than ourselves which some people call God. It will also mean discipline and some practice of habitual prayer. And by prayer, I mean only a simple and honest reaching out of the human heart toward whatever power there may be at the foundation of life. Of course I can't prove there is a God. But even at the rational level, I think the existence of this world makes more sense with a God than without one. I believe there is an afterlife, and the way we live in this world will affect the way we will live there.

I do not censure or condemn those who do not or cannot believe in God. I say only that faith is a gift, that I am a believer, and pray I remain so until my earthly end. I cannot put it better than Morris West, who wrote, "I have learned to be grateful for the small candle that lights my faltering steps and hope that when it gutters out, I may wake to a final illumination."

2

My Love Affair with Radio
(Unpublished)

When I was growing up we didn't have a radio in our home. I'm not sure why. It wasn't as if my father couldn't afford one. He was careful with the family budget, but he certainly could have bought us a radio. Why didn't he? I think it had something to do with our religious background and my father's attitude to some elements of Catholicism. We were staunch Irish Roman Catholics living in a strong, loyal Orange Protestant community. Liberal in many ways, my father had developed a puritanical, almost a Jansenist virus, in some of his religious attitudes. Dancing and films were, depending on the circumstances, suspect; so was the radio, because radio, in my father's view, brought with it a nonspiritual, materialistic, even anti-religious message that my dad considered dangerous.

The event that changed his position was the fact that the local radio station began to carry some religious programs, and strongly Roman Catholic to boot. Who can forget the impact of Monsignor Fulton J. Sheen who began broadcasting in the 1930s, and later made the transition to television where he became so popular he dethroned Milton Berle as the king of television. In any event, I have Monsignor Sheen to thank for introducing me

Neil McKenty in 1941, a student at Campbellford High School

to radio. I can still feel the hair standing on the back of my head as I recall his mellifluous voice reverberating around our modest living room. Mind you, our radio listening was severely rationed.

But as Christmas approached, I no longer had to sneak over to the neighbours to listen to the T. Eaton holiday programs which led up to the department store's annual Santa Claus Parade.

Soon there was another program, which my father never missed: Father Charles Coughlin, "the radio priest," altogether quite another cup of tea. Every Sunday afternoon my dad turned on the radio to hear Coughlin's orotund velvet tones. He had a voice like an organ, soothing, rich, mesmerizing, and he played with your emotions the way a maestro conducts an orchestra.

The trouble was not Father Coughlin. It was his message. His world view was straight forward enough: the world was run by a small clique of men. (I am positive there were no women in the group) whom Coughlin called "international bankers," most of whom were Jews. If only we could smash these Jewish lackeys and their communist fellow travellers, the Kingdom of Peace, Justice, and of Jesus Christ would emerge on earth. If these remarkable Catholics – Mussolini, Hitler, and Franco – could smash the dirty Jewish conspiracy, that was fine with Coughlin. When you stripped away all the religious veneer, what you discovered was that Coughlin was a small-bore fascist, a bigot, and a full-fledged anti-Semite.

My father was a fair man and he was not a bigot. But he believed that the big shots of this world walked all over the little guy, and there was little justice for those who did not have a big bank balance. If Coughlin was for the underdog, whatever that meant, that was all right with my dad. We continued to listen faithfully every Sunday, until Coughlin was taken off the air by his own religious superiors for his inflammatory statements.

It was during Father Coughlin's heyday that my interest in print and broadcast media began to grow. As long as I can remember I have always been interested in writing. In 1936 I wrote a long essay on the Spanish Civil War. I admit, I defended

Franco because all of the Catholics I knew, including my parents, were praying that he would defeat the godless communists. Shortly after I began classes at Campbellford High School, where my English teacher, Kate Ferris, a tall, angular spinster who taught the parsing of sentences as others might teach figure skating, stopped beside my desk one day and said, "You should work at your writing. You have a flair for it."

When I was 15, the *Peterborough Examiner* was looking for a stringer. And I was asked if I was interested in the job. I jumped at the chance. Being a newspaper stringer in Hastings was like being a minnow in the Trent River. But that wasn't the point. Its editor was Robertson Davies (who went on to become one of Canada's literary giants.) I covered village council meetings, sports events, traffic accidents, fires, runaway horses, Sunday afternoon teas, and lawn bowling tournaments. I was paid ten cents a column inch for hard news, such as a fisherman from Ohio catching a record-breaking muskellunge, or three cents a column inch for the personal stuff (Mrs. Stubbs and Mrs. Turner.) As soon as I was old enough to drive I bought an old Dodge touring car for thirty dollars, in partnership with my closest friend, Tim Coughlan. The car, whose leaking gas tank we tried to patch with bubble gum, had an enormous windshield. I went to the *Hastings Star* and ordered a large sign which I attached to the windshield. It read: PRESS. Everyone in Hastings and environs knew I was the local reporter for the *Examiner.*

From the Hastings Star, 1939
Now the Words Live

His Majesty King George reads carefully and well. When he was searching for material for his Christmas Day Broadcast to the Empire he "came across" something which impressed him and he decided to use it. Here it is:

"I said to the man who stood at the gate of the year, 'Give me a light that I may tread safely into the unknown,' and he replied, "Go out into the darkness and put your hand in the hand of God. That shall be to you better than a light and safer than a known way."

And then the search was on. No authority came forth to name the author of those words. When literary critics, librarians and all such were asked regarding the author, they began speaking about Chesterton, Rudyard Kipling, John Bunyan, but they found nothing. Heads of universities in several places and in several nations admitted they were stumped; it was not until an anonymous telephone call reached the British Broadcasting Corporation that the much desired information was received. It was found they were written by Miss Minnie Louise Haskins and were published in a letter in the *London Times* shortly before 1914. Apparently lost and hidden in the interval, they were selected by His Majesty for the conclusion of his message to his people in troubled days.

One frigid afternoon in 1940 I learned that the first young man from Hastings had been killed in the war. Bud Richardson had been a star athlete before he went into the Air Force. His death in action was a terrible blow to our little town. I grabbed my notebook and walked the three miles to the home of Bud Richardson's parents. I talked to them about their son and borrowed their only picture of him in uniform. Bud's death in action and his picture and his story in the *Examiner*, brought the impact of the war home to Hastings in a personal way. And I recorded it. An experience I will never forget.

Then there was a third name in my radio logs: Walter Winchell. Winchell was a potent mix of Ann Landers and Al Capone. His delivery on radio resembled the sound of a continuous round of shots from a high powered rifle. As soon as he ended his broadcast, I would pick up one of his newspaper columns and try my level best to imitate his delivery. That continued until my father roared down from his upstairs bedroom that I should cease and desist because my infernal racket was keeping the household from its sleep. I considered his reprimand a minor price to pay for the rush I got pretending to be the best radio broadcaster of the day. Nor was my father too pleased when I ran away from home to become a radio star. In this case running away meant taking the bus to Peterborough to talk my way into a job with radio station CHEX and convince the program director to let me audition. I must have been all of 16. The program director was kind enough to say that I had a certain amount of talent and advised me to come back when I finished my education.

In fact, I didn't go back. It was almost 15 years later when I had the chance to do live radio, and I jumped at it. By that time my father was dead, I was a Jesuit priest teaching at Regiopolis College where I introduced a new element to the school's debating society – mock parliaments. It worked so well that the local radio station, CKWS, invited us to broadcast one of our sessions. That nourished, briefly, my continuing interest in radio. As a priest, I learned to appreciate the clarity and the precision of Latin. I believe that the study of the classics helped me to frame questions and conduct conversations that were both logical and orderly. Anyone who knows Latin, or the classical thesis method, can develop the status quaestionis, or summary, of the topic under discussion, and I believe can think more clearly.

A lot of water went under the dam before my next experience with radio. I was ordained in 1957, took graduate degrees in history and communication arts, and worked with the Jesuits in New York and in London before I decided to leave the priesthood. After that, I spent two years working with Harry Red Foster and the Kennedy Foundation on the Special Olympics for the mentally challenged as the first executive director of the Foster Foundation. Working with Red Foster was like working for a threshing machine. There were speeches to write (and sometimes deliver), meetings to attend, and sometimes to organize.

Red Foster, the Kennedys, and the Special Olympics

The highlight of my time with Red Foster was not rubbing elbows with big name people. It was being involved with the intellectually handicapped themselves. One event stands out – the first Canadian National Special Olympics which were held at the CNE and Ontario Place in June, 1971. Enormous preparations had gone into organizing these games and teams from all ten provinces had been entered.

On a warm June evening, the opening ceremonies took place on the track in front of the grandstand. There they all were, the dignitaries, the Lieutenant-Governor in his gold braid, the premier, city officials, military aides in their glittering uniforms, bands, and cheerleaders. Then I looked down the track. A band came into view. Next, from each of the ten provinces, then came the flag bearers and behind them the special athletes, carrying in their hearts their special oath, "Let me win, but if I cannot win, let me be brave in the attempt." Some of them stumbled a bit, some of them hobbled, still others tried to do a little jig, but all of them beamed and waved and smiled in a kind of happy benediction. I smiled back. I, also handicapped in my own halting way, tried to reach out to them, to respond to their courage. And I started to cry.

Then, sometime in 1972, I concluded that my work with the Foster Foundation was winding down, and I began a leisurely search for a new job. One morning, as I was lackadaisically reading the business section of the *Globe and Mail*, my eye caught a rather large advertisement for a "Director of Public Affairs for a large metropolitan radio station." There was no mention of the city, but the ad said a background in history and an interest in current affairs were required. I applied. It turned out the position was with CJAD in Montreal. The station needed to replace its Director of Public Affairs, Rod Blaker, because he was leaving to run for the Liberal Party in the 1972 federal election. I won the position over 60 other applicants.

Day One at CJAD

On the first Monday of October, I walked, with a degree of uncertainty, through the doors of CJAD, which at that time was at the corner of Mountain and Ste. Catherine Streets, across from Ogilvy's Department Store. I was expected to go on the air that very day to begin pontificating to the largest English-speaking audience. I begged Bill Hambly, the station manager, to give me a few days to get myself oriented. He was adamant. I was to get myself into the studio and in front of microphone and start talking that very day. I have no idea what I said in my first broadcast. I will be frank – most of my editorials were about subjects I knew nothing about. I knew a great deal more about Toronto than I did about Montreal.

In terms of radio, my first few years were not especially memorable or inspiring. Each day I would read three or four newspapers desperately searching for material on which to write an editorial. I developed a moderate, liberal position on most issues, including the importance of the French language in Quebec. That left me open to being called a weakling, a quisling, and a closet separatist, which is how I was often branded by the neighbourhood weekly newspaper, the *Suburban*. I never minded the criticism as long as they spelled my name correctly.

I also took a hard line on two other controversial issues – abortion and capital punishment. I was against both. This gives me the opportunity to make two points. First, at the time I used tactics not unlike Father Coughlin, which I wish I had not employed. My editorials were almost inflammatory and were not appropriate. I think they were giving vent to some subconscious stream of my own anger. I was, however, convinced that the controversy I engendered improved ratings. I still believe that it does. But the price you pay, and ask others to pay, ruins your credibility. I would not do commentaries of that nature again, although I still oppose abortion and capital punishment

Neil with Prime Minister Pierre Trudeau
at Maple Leaf Gardens in Toronto, 1971.

CANADA

PRIME MINISTER · PREMIER MINISTRE

O T T A W A (K1A 0A2),
July 7, 1971.

Dear Mr. McKenty:

      My staff has advised me of the
splendid job you did in making arrangements
for my visit to the Special Olympics for
the Mentally Retarded.

      I would like you to know that I
thoroughly enjoyed the event and very much
appreciated all your efforts in making it
the complete success that it was.

Sincerely,

Mr. Neil McKenty,
    Executive Director,
       Foster Foundation,
          Foster Building,
            40 St. Clair Avenue,
              Toronto, Ontario.

I also took a hard line on two other controversial issues – abortion and capital punishment. I was against both. This gives me the opportunity to make two points. First, at the time I used tactics not unlike Father Coughlin, which I wish I had not employed. My editorials were almost inflammatory and were not appropriate. I think they were giving vent to some subconscious stream of my own anger. I was, however, convinced that the controversy I engendered improved ratings. I still believe that it does. But the price you pay, and ask others to pay, ruins your credibility. I would not do commentaries of that nature again, although I still oppose abortion and capital punishment

> *I am opposed to abortion because I think an attack on life at any stage threatens life at every stage. You don't need to be a rocket scientist to know that life begins at conception. The Pope has a perfect right to condemn abortion. His condemnation of Catholic politicians who support policies like abortion and same-sex marriage is more problematic. After all, our politicians swear to uphold the Constitution of Canada, not the Catechism of the Catholic Church.*
>
> *There are only two arguments that can be made in favour of capital punishment. One, that it is a deterrent or revenge, "An eye for an eye and a tooth for a tooth." There is absolutely no evidence to show that hanging a man deters crime, which leaves revenge. I don't see how any country that calls itself civilized can base its public policy on revenge or vengeance. Justice that kills is not justice at all.*

Which brings me to my second point: the freedom that CJAD allowed me to express my views. I am sure some of my commentaries made the station management uncomfortable. But I was never hauled onto the carpet for doing what I had been paid to do. Even when some commercial sponsors complained and demanded that I be reined in or fired, I was never instructed to tone down my positions. This is a tribute to the integrity and to the liberalism of CJAD and its management team. I doubt I would have had the same editorial freedom at many other stations.

Shortly after arriving I became responsible for another program, "Prime Time," which was directed at seniors. It became a gem of a show, and it really jelled when we convinced Edgar Andrew Collard, who wrote a weekly historical column for the *Gazette*, to participate. Collard would come in every few weeks and tape about eight segments which offered an interesting glimpse into the city's history. These vignettes added an authentic Montreal flavour to the show and gave me the opportunity to interview the most informed raconteur of Montreal's story then alive.

It must have been in 1975, less than two years after my career in radio began, that suddenly it appeared, my broadcasting days were over. I was informed by the station manager, Bill Hambly, that I had been fired. I was not to show up at the station the next day. What a stunner.

Hambly was by no means thoughtless or cruel. He did his best to explain why he was letting me go. The station had hired a veteran radio personality, John Robertson, to do editorial commentaries. And they had promoted another radio veteran, Ted Blackman, to be program director. Blackman had made it a condition of his acceptance that I be dumped. I am not sure why this was so. Blackman's real forte was sports, not public affairs. Hambly explained, as kindly as he could, that he had no choice but to let me go.

I kept on talking. I explained that I had left Toronto to set up living arrangements in Montreal and had not been given a fair shot. I argued that if I could stay, I would show him that I could make a contribution and somehow get around the Blackman problem. I was desperate to hang on to the job. The meeting with Hambly ended in a kind of verbal murkiness. Everything was left up in the air, but the door was closed.

I took advantage of his ambiguity and walked into the station the following Monday to host "Prime Time." No one threw me out. (Blackman eventually killed the show. He thought it gave the station too old an image.)

Luckily for me, Montreal was beginning to gear up for the 1976 Olympics and somehow I managed to insinuate myself into the team for Olympic coverage. It was around this time that I had my first encounter with Mayor Jean Drapeau. I was part of a three-man panel interviewing the mayor about Olympic planning. The three of us gave the mayor a rough time, but he never lost his sense of humour. During a commercial break, he turned to me and said that as soon as we opened the telephone lines, the tables would turn and the joke would be on us. The public would support him. He was right. It did. I recall we took about 17 calls, and 13 of them supported him down the line.

3

CJAD's First-ever Open-line Talk Show
by Neil McKenty

Covering the Olympics was an exciting adventure. It was a great time to be in Montreal and to be on radio. One of my indelible memories is strolling down to the Montreal Forum one night to watch gymnast Nadia Comaneci score a perfect ten. I was on the phone and on the air within ten seconds. Blackman and I never became pals, but I believe he began to respect me.

One day he called me into his office, sat me down, and asked me if I would be interested in becoming moderator of CJAD's first-ever open-line talk show. I nearly fell off my chair. The program would run from 10 to 11 a.m., five days a week, and my co-host would be Hélène Gougeon, a seasoned professional. (Her husband was the distinguished author, playwright, and Laurier biographer, Joseph Schull,) I was startled by Blackman's offer, because I didn't think he had that much confidence in me, and I certainly didn't have that much confidence in me. Doing a daily talk show in Montreal, with all its conflicting and treacherous undercurrents, seemed to me a daunting prospect.

The day before the show was to debut Elvis Presley died. I say this not because I was a fan of Presley, but because his death was the topic of my first "Exchange" program. Normally, I would not have chosen Presley, but Montreal was going nuts over his premature death of a drug overdose. There were candle light vigils and special charter flights to take fans to his funeral in Tennessee. I couldn't ignore the impact of Presley's passing. I did the only thing I could do. I took a contrarian view. I switched on the microphone and openly questioned why there was so much fuss over the death of an overweight, bloated, pill-popping singer with rotten teeth. You can guess what happened. The lines melted with outrage. The response was exactly what I had wanted. It demonstrated that (a) I had a lot of listeners, (b) many of them were young, which was great for advertising sales, and (c) any self doubt I may have had about generating calls was unfounded. The lines opened and kept blazing for the next ten years.

Thanks to my enthusiastic and intelligent producer, Trish McKenna and Holly Haimerl, it became one of the most exciting in the business – being plugged into a Montreal audience for two hours. We talked about everything from abortion to incest. One of the zaniest shows I recall was "Driving With Your Mate,"– (neilmckenty.com/radio) – how to get along with your spouse while driving a car. Live radio is simultaneously exhilarating, intimate, anonymous, and enormously flexible.

The program which provoked the most uproar involved Brian Mulroney when he was still leader of Her Majesty's Opposition. He agreed to be a guest on the program, but his handlers informed me that one of the conditions of his coming on "Exchange" was that he would not take any telephone calls. To me, that made as much sense as going for a television interview on the condition that no one turn on the lights. The *Toronto Star* got wind of Mulroney's conditions, carried the story on its front page, and by the time he arrived at CJAD he was in a rage. I was ordered to the station manager's office.

There was Mulroney, perspiring, red-faced, and yelling at me for embarrassing him politically. "Why should I waste my time taking calls from English-speaking Montrealers?" he shouted, "They are all bloody Liberals."

But Mulroney was no fool. He knew that he had more to lose than to gain if he ducked the questions. So he stood up, squared his shoulders, flashed a wan smile, and went on the air. He took a dozen or so calls, almost all of them in his favour. Callers gave him both a warm and an intelligent reception. Brian's political instincts were typically sound when he took the calls. His visit to "Exchange" received wide and favourable coverage. I didn't see Mulroney again until after he became Prime Minister. We had a warm, friendly conversation at the St. Patrick's Ball. I heard him turn to Brian Gallery, the Mayor of Westmount and one of his cronies, and say "I think McKenty has mellowed."

Mulroney later sent Neil a letter, and as a post-script added, "As a shareholder, I urge you to keep those ratings high!"

The most rewarding episode of my radio career, however, had to do with a taxi driver, Marcel Belisle, who had been awarded a medal for bravery. He had jumped into the cab of an empty runaway truck which was rolling towards a school bus loaded with children. He somehow managed to wrestle the truck to a stop before it hit the bus. But in the process, he was injured and could no longer work. He had the medal, but no money. I told his story on the air, opened up the lines, and within two hours had collected $11,700 in pledges.

I remain convinced that if one has to do radio, a live talk show is the way to go, and for me at any rate, CJAD, at the heart of the magic city of Montreal, is the best place to do it. Political, ethical, religious, and scientific topics can be discussed on the air in informative and entertaining ways. Insulting listeners and callers alike, which is the stock in trade of shock jocks, is not typical of talk radio. And in Montreal we had the ratings to prove it.

4

City's Talk Show Host
Isn't Full of Hot Air

Mike Boone, *The Gazette*, July 23, 1983

Montreal radio phone-in shows have always burned up the airways with fire-breathing demagoguery. And then there is Neil McKenty – historian, biographer, former priest, and good listener. McKenty is the voice of moderation, a man whose personality is anything but that of a stereotypical phone-in host. In the years McKenty has been on the air, "Exchange" has become Montreal's most popular English language phone-in program – success which the host attributes to "the quality of our callers and the respect with which we treat them. We invite people to call "Exchange," says McKenty, "They're our guests while they are on the program. It would be pretty bloody cheeky of me to invite someone to be my guest and then dump all over them in the first minute. My proclivity is to be on the patient side.

"In the years I have been doing the show," McKenty said, "I've become less obtrusive in every respect – the amount of time I talk, the vigor with which I express opinions. I see "Exchange" as an information program with a high entertainment quotient. I've never wanted to do it as a classical hot-line show." McKenty's steadfast refusal to become ringmaster of a radio three-ring circus owes as much to his own upbringing and personality as it does do his conviction that "hot-line is passé." In a radio world dominated by gigantic egos and ruthless ambition, he is an anomaly. "I got into the media quite late," McKenty says. "There was never any time when I wanted to run a radio station. If I were 25 it might be a different ball game. But I have no goals. I am enjoying life where I am. I am doing what I want to do at a station where they let me do it. Maybe it is because of my Jesuit background or growing up in the latter years of the Depression, but money is not something I think about." For two hours every morning McKenty has numerous occasions to tell his listeners "the lines are blazing."

"Exchange" has been a consistent ratings winner. Al Pervin, host of CFCF's "In Conversation" attributes McKenty's success to two factors: "McKenty has a fatherly image," says Pervin, currently anchorman of a CBC television newscast in New Brunswick. "That type of character personified by Walter Cronkite is very hard to project successfully. The other thing is his consistency. McKenty is always right there in a consistent format which people rely on and learn to trust." Once callers get through to the host, they are assured of ample opportunity to state their cases without getting involved in a screaming match with McKenty. During the planning for what McKenty called "a reluctant experiment" in which a psychic would be invited as a guest, he made it clear to his producer that no callers asking personal questions would be tolerated. "This show might be entertaining," said McKenty, "but we are not going to have poor, misbegotten souls phoning in to ask if they should move to Edmonton."

The discipline of his previous experience as an historical biographer is evident in McKenty's approach to his work on "Exchange." He arrives at the studios week day mornings at 8 a.m. to begin two hours of preparation for the day's "Exchange." "I can't remember a day in the last six years when I have gone into the station reluctantly," says McKenty. "Callers would pick it up quickly if I were taking a cynical approach to my job. I am sure there are people who … switch the dial because they can't stand me. But what they get on "Exchange" is Neil McKenty – the genuine article. That's not what they get on a lot of talk shows."

5

Neil McKenty and the Intriguing Case of Marcel Belisle

The fact that Neil's most memorable radio moment sprang from the story of a Montreal cab driver and the community that reached out to help him should come as no surprise. Neil never believed his calling to be simply to provide a forum for high-profile politicians and other well-connected individuals to voice their opinions. For Neil, the real power in radio was its ability to bring people together, to build community, to create a place where everyday folks could connect, a place where they could feel comfortable expressing what was on their mind. His job, as Neil so often said, was to stay out of the way.

Such was the case with Marcel Belisle, the Montreal cab driver whose few moments of fame would cost him three years of grief. It was on the morning of February 21, 1973, that the 36-year-old Belisle noticed a large tractor-trailer moving alongside him down St. Urbain St. What he saw next, however, was beyond belief. There was no driver in the truck! Belisle quickly jumped from his taxi into the cab of the runaway truck only to discover that neither the air brakes nor the emergency brake were working.

After a harrowing drive that at times reached speeds of 50 miles per hour, Belisle, in spectacular fashion, stopped the runaway truck from plunging into traffic where it would almost certainly have killed people. In the process, Belisle fractured his pelvis, suffered cuts and bruises and lost two of his teeth.

Now unable to work, life became difficult for Belisle. The trucking company refused to provide him with any compensation, telling him the truck would have stopped on its own and that he was to blame for his own injuries. To make matters worse Belisle was not eligible for unemployment insurance, nor could he receive workmen's compensation.

As time went by, things got worse. In order to provide for his family Belisle mortgaged his house while he convalesced. On December 13, 1974, Belisle was presented with the Star of Courage by Governor-General Jules Leger for what was termed to be an act of conspicuous bravery performed in circumstances of great peril. In 1976 the Montreal Citizenship Council honoured him with the title of Outstanding Citizen. The honours kept coming, but they didn't pay the bills. Neil believed society owed a debt to Belisle. He launched a radio appeal for help and within three hours collected more than $11,000 in pledges.

Within a week of working with Neil, I became fascinated with his orderly thinking, his meticulous preparation for even the most light-hearted subjects. He respects his audience and that is what eventually surfaces. It is not surprising that his is one of the most listened to programs on Montreal radio. Sure, he's aggravating but that seems to stimulate people to engage in our discussions. You have to be impressed with his intellect and his innate kindness.
–Hélène Gougeon, quoted by Joan Capreol Westmount Examiner,
June 2, 1978.

Graceful, thoughtful, of clear mind – the kind of guy who knew the difference between right and wrong. He was not a guy that really sounded off an awful lot about what he was going to say, but when

he got into the studio and turned the mike on, and he said it, he got your attention.
–Ric Peterson, who worked with Neil at CJAD

I invite people to call. They are my guests while they are on the program. It would be pretty bloody cheeky of me to invite someone to be a guest, then dump all over them in the first minute. I tend to be patient. In the years I have been doing the show I have learned to become much less obtrusive in every respect – in the amount of time I talk, and in the vigor with which I express opinions. It is the kind of show only radio can do, and on almost every program I learn something from the listeners. I see "Exchange" as an information program with a high entertainment content.
–Neil McKenty

The show seemed spontaneous and freewheeling, but generally speaking each "Exchange" was planned a week in advance. Neil and his producer, Holly Haimerl, were methodical in their approach. They worked hard to prevent the show from being monotonous. Getting through to Neil on the air was not simply a matter of dialing 790-0991. Before guests were put on the air, callers were asked what they intended to discuss, and calls that were not relevant to the topic of the day were weeded out. Haimerl looked for a balance between young and old, male and female, and those callers who could balance opinion, both pro and con. Regular callers were restricted to phoning in once a week. Those who did manage to get through were allowed to state their case without getting into a shouting match with each other. Callers were discouraged from asking personal questions. The show was flexible, and catered to a wide variety of listeners, including topics that were of particular interest to seniors. He relied heavily on the news department, which often provided him with ideas for the program. He made two trips for CJAD: one to the Middle East visiting Egypt, Syria, and Israel, and one to Washington, DC to cover the Watergate hearings.

I invite people to call.
They are my guests while they are on the program.

6

Phone-in Radio Is the Talk of the Town

Special to *The Gazette*
Juan Rodriguez, Saturday, Sept. 13, 1980

People say the darndest things, and one of the best places in the world to hear people talk, babble, argue, and complain in two languages is Montreal. It has no fewer than 14 daily phone-in radio programs. The moderators earn up to $40,000 a year for encouraging, putting up with, and cutting off approximately 250,000 callers. How about this from "Exchange" on CJAD?

Hello Neil, how are you?

Fine, go ahead, you are on the air.

Neil, just one point, have you ever noticed the uncanny resemblance between Abraham Lincoln and Claude Ryan? (a journalist who was then leader of the Quebec Liberal Party). You know, the hooked nose, the deep sunken eyes….

No sir, it never struck me. Well it struck *ME*.

Some 55,000 anglophones demonstrate that they are a highly vocal minority on Neil McKenty's "Exchange," and jock hustler, Ted Tevan, bullies callers to CFCF on *Sports Rap* for another 30,000 listeners. About 5,000 insomniacs, lonely hearts, and night birds while away the wee hours on CFCF's "Night Talk."

Hot-line shows are so popular that even CBM, the local CBC station near the bottom of audience ratings, gets most of its listeners when it opens the airwaves on "Radio Noon." Montreal carved a niche in hot-line history with two of the most abrasive phonein hosts ever: Pat Burns and Joe Pyne, popular in the 1950s and 1960s. "Unpredictable" is the best word to describe the way callers approach topics for discussion. Some people are regulars who leap to the phones before the issue of the day is announced. They call out of loneliness, outrage, and a desire to be heard.

Poignant, pugnacious people have opinions on everything. Controversy runs rampant. Have you had problems enrolling your children in English school? Had any hassles baptizing your infant? Are civil servants paid too much? Should women have to admit their age on official documents? Should the Klu Klux Klan be allowed to set up an office in Toronto? Should boxing be banned? Would you rather live in another country? And there are always callers with fixations on the resemblance between Abe Lincoln and Claude Ryan.

McKenty, a former Jesuit, looks as though he'd be at home thundering from a pulpit. On the air he is parental in a dithering way. McKenty professes peaceful co-existence with callers. He points to the ratings as vindication of his approach, but his exchanges can be sharp. Recently, McKenty asked," Do we really love our country?"

A slew of folks called in to answer yes, but one immigrant put it succinctly: I am sick of hearing of the mother country. We should leave the mother country alone and work to make Canada beautiful. "Good point" offers McKenty. Why should we always be muling and puking about the mother country? The difference between Canadians and Americans, the caller says, is that while it is difficult to find an American who cannot belt out the "Stars and Stripes," Canadians seem reluctant to sing "O Canada" because, he reasons, we don't know the words.

By now the lines are blazing, and a caller gets on who strikes a raw nerve. "I would like to offer a somewhat negative opinion of

Canada. I came here from Ireland, about 22 years ago, and I'm a musician, eh, and I played this function at the Ritz Carlton, and these Americans had no problem bursting into their anthem. Why can't Canadians do it? Maybe it's because the country is so dull. I get a little tired of people saying how great it is….."

"Well," huffs McKenty, "I get a little more tired of people saying what a crock it is."

"Maybe if we had a war," says the Irish guy "we'd have more character."

McKenty cuts him off, something he rarely does.

"Normally, I don't consider my callers as enemies, and I don't describe "Exchange" as a hot-line show. The primary purpose is to give listeners an opportunity to reply to each other, not to me. Indeed, I am stimulated by them. I usually leave the show more refreshed than when I started.

He always says he never gets to know any of his callers personally. "It's not something I encourage," and he doesn't hear a peep from his Westmount neighbours "My wife hears from them though."

7

"The Zaniest Show I Ever Did"

No one in talk radio knows for certain what will resonate with listeners. Or why. To Neil's consternation and surprise, one of his most popular "Exchange" programs was "Driving With your Mate." These are his crib notes for the program, which elicited comments from callers for two months running.

Did you ever get lost, really lost? How did you get unlost?

Why are male drivers reluctant to ask directions?

Are men better than women at driving? I know my own wife, Catharine, gives up as a map reader and as a navigator at least once on every trip we take.

Do you think men change personalities when they get behind the wheel?

I do most of the driving in my family. I consider myself a good driver, and I am uncomfortable with someone else behind the wheel. I wonder why that is? I don't like driving with drivers I don't know. It makes me nervous. I feel more comfortable behind the wheel than sitting in the passenger seat.

There is something darn funny about how a car affects people. Why do we always pack so much luggage? Going let's say, to Rawdon, we have enough luggage in the trunk to go on a cruise around the world on the Queen Mary. Why do we need so much luggage?

Catharine's reply:

> *The darling man was directionally challenged, Known to go through the occasional stop sign or red light unless the navigator, me, could stop him. Never a dull moment! The luggage, on the other hand, was mostly mine, and never ceased to amaze him. Can you believe we made it?*

8

Cats!

In the early 1970s, Neil and Catharine moved into a small, unpretentious house at 66 Somerville Ave. in lower Westmount, the area that is now called Victoria Village. His backyard was connected to Terry Mosher's backyard, separated only by a waist-high rickety, wooden fence. The Gazette's provocative editorial cartoonist, otherwise known as Aislin, learned that even rickety fences do make good neighbours.

They were the best of neighbours. The McKentys were recent arrivals from Ontario apparently, truly an oddity in those politically-charged days when Quebec was flexing its nationalistic muscles. Little did I know that Neil was about to become the host of a phone-in show on CJAD, Montreal's most popular English language radio station. We had many animated conversations over our shared back fence, agreeing on most points during those heady days of the Quebec government's adoption of Bill 101 and the election of René Lévesque and the Parti Québécois. Back then, I must admit to only listening to the radio occasionally – usually while fishing about, trying to come up with a cartoon idea. There is no better forum to discover what people are concerned with than on live talk shows. Now, one day I was listening in to Neil's show when he began talking about his back garden, a truly comfortable hideout with a lot of plant life and shrubbery, most of it courtesy of Catharine I would suspect. Neil was going on about how much he loved the many birds that were attracted to their garden. The problem was that the birds were being harassed by a number of cats.

"I hate cats," Neil said – right there on CJAD.

Well. The nerve! At the time, my then wife and I owned eight cats.

In a huff, I immediately called Neil on air.

"Welcome, Terry!" he said, in most effusive manner. "Never mind that, Neil," I responded, "I don't want anything happening to my cats! If anything does, there is going to be a lot of trouble."

I then hung up – but continued to listen in.

So began a cavalcade of calls to Neil, mostly from what sounded like nice little old ladies, all defending their dear little pussycats. There was no stopping them – call after call. After an hour or so of this, Neil surrendered: "Could we PLEASE talk about something other than cats!" he pleaded.

All of this started a nice little tradition: for years after that, Neil and I would exchange Christmas cards – all of them containing images of cats in one form or another.

No birds.

The next morning the door bell rang and Terry presented Neil with the original of his cat cartoon. Much to Neil's delight. It has hung in a place of honour for many a year. Meantime, a family of five squirrels maintained their right of residence in Neil and Catharine's garden (with its apple trees), turning somersaults for no good reason, but under the watchful eyes of Terry's cats.

One day a caller complained to Neil on air that the Gazette had changed its type and he could no longer read the obituary columns. Neil said he couldn't do anything about the problem, and suggested that everyone who agreed with the caller and had problems reading the paper should complain to The Gazette. Those were the days when the newspaper still had a switchboard.

The receptionists were swamped. McKenty wasn't the most popular person around the newspaper that day.

9

Politics
by Neil McKenty

Neil arrived on air just as Quebec nationalism began to percolate. The Parti Québécois was elected in 1976 and shortly after that, Premier René Lévesque held a referendum on sovereignty. Neil was convinced that no matter what happened, those who spoke English had a role to play in Quebec.

Quebec's English Community

When you're on the firing line you're bound to take a lot of flak. Is there any group in Canada that's more on the firing line than the English community in Montreal? And is there any group that gets more advice about what we should do.? Some say we are not wanted here. We should pick up our marbles and leave. Others say this is our home. We should hit the streets and fight. In fact, with few exceptions, the English community has done neither. In a time of extreme pressure the English community has kept its cool. It's still here. It hasn't gone off half-cocked. It has retained its fundamental common sense. We haven't been panicked by the confusion of events. We haven't been driven away by insults. And we haven't followed false prophets.

The English community rejected English separation out of hand. Others told us we had to grab on to the hands of the clock and force them back. They offered us a pig in a poke and they called it a choice. It was, in fact, an illusion. I think it is high time we recognized the qualities the English community in Quebec has displayed in this time of change. The English community deserves credit for its maturity and its balance. It also deserves the credit for refusing to be seduced by simple solutions. It refused to join groups that wanted to turn the clock back in Quebec. Some of the qualities of Quebec's English community were recalled at a meeting of the Canadian Club. The chairman of the Positive Action Committee, Alex Paterson, doesn't try to turn the clock back. He urges the English community to stay and play its full role in the new and changing Quebec. Mr. Paterson has two arguments for remaining in Quebec. First the names and the history of the English community in this province, names like McGill, the Royal Victoria Hospital, Osler, Penfield, Norman Bethune, Hugh McLennan, Mordecai Richler, and Frank Scott. We shouldn't give up easily what our forefathers created here.

Secondly, at the time of the referendum, Quebec will need every person who believes in Canada. Mr. Paterson announced that the Pro-Canada Committee will be fighting the referendum street by street. Many members of the English community are fighting now as members of pro-federalist political parties. You don't hear from these people. They aren't yelling. They aren't leaving. They aren't depending on simple solutions. They are members of the English-speaking community, and they are quietly working with their French-speaking federalist counterparts for a new Quebec in a united Canada.

They deserve our thanks.

During the debate over Quebec sovereignty Neil was empathetic when emotions on both sides were highly charged. CBC Broadcaster Bernard St. Laurent, who was then CJAD's Quebec legislative reporter, points out that while McKenty was a passionate Canadian, he was not as intense in his opposition to the Parti Québécois as those English speaking Quebecers who were born and bred in Quebec.

Neil had no preconceived notions about Quebec politics. I recall that, after the 1980 Quebec referendum, conventional wisdom, especially among the English-speaking pundits, was that Liberal Opposition Leader Claude Ryan would defeat René Lévesque in the provincial election which followed. It seemed to be wishful thinking. To put it in context: the Parti Québécois held a referendum looking for a mandate to negotiate Quebec's sovereignty with the rest of Canada. Claude Ryan vigorously campaigned against the idea. So when the PQ lost the 1980 referendum, and lost badly, it was assumed that Ryan would go on to win the next provincial election. Ryan appeared on Neil's show during the election campaign and warned listeners that Lévesque would call a snap election on sovereignty in two or three years if his mandate was renewed. Ryan suggested that holding referendums until they finally won one "appears to be the PQ's new tactic after the failure of the 1980 referendum."

But it seemed to me that, just because Quebecers voted no to sovereignty, it didn't mean they didn't like Lévesque's government. I had a nagging feeling that the strength of the Liberal Party, and Ryan's popularity in particular, had been exaggerated. I told Neil about my reservations and suggested the two of us get out of the West Island, go to Galleries D'Anjou in east end Montreal, and take a poll on our own to plumb the depths of Quebec nationalism. So off we went to talk to the burghers in the east end, lugging our big Sony TC-142 three-headed tape recorders with us. I went down one side of the mall and Neil went down the other. We asked people how they planned to vote. After about an hour we met to compare notes. "Jesus Christ, Bernie," Neil exclaimed, "the PQ is going to win!" And win they did, taking the highest percentage of the votes in the party's history. Lévesque was returned with 80 seats and 49 per cent of the vote.

Ryan took 46 per cent of the vote, which gave him 42 seats.

Premier René Lévesque understood Neil's influence with English-speaking Quebecers, corresponded with Neil, and appeared on "Exchange" several times.

GOUVERNEMENT DU QUÉBEC
LE PREMIER MINISTRE

Québec, May 30th, 1984

Mr. Neil McKenty
Director of Public Affairs
CJAD 800
1411 rue du Fort
Montréal, Qué. H3H 2R1

Dear Mr. McKenty,

Thank you for your letter of May 14th,
enclosing your Editorial following the tragic shooting in
the National Assembly.

It was reassuring to have your comments
expressing genuine respect for democratic institutions. I am
sure too your listeners agreed with you in your denunciation
of violence, in all its forms, as a means of expressing an
opinion or disapproval.

Again thanking you for your kind expression
of sympathy.

Yours very truly,

René Lévesque

The regular listeners to McKenty's show rarely got the opportunity to hear a classic exchange in which the caller gets under the skin of both the host and his guest. Talk shows are usually manipulated to uphold the opinions of the moderator, and anyone with a contrary opinion is given a fast shuffle. Not so with Neil. The following transcript is of a broadcast in which Neil had as his guest the Gazette's publisher Clark W. Davey. The Gazette had printed an editorial suggesting that the English-speaking minority in Quebec might have to surrender some rights to broker linguistic peace and to guarantee French-language supremacy in the province.

CALLER: You made remarks Mr. Davey concerning the future of *The Gazette*, which if I remember correctly, you stated had a responsibility to "other areas than the English milieu here in Montreal and the province." This attitude, I think, was what contributed to the diminishing of the English community in this province, because it suggests that the English don't have complete rights to their own language and culture here, but rather, that the future of the English here was inevitably towards integration.

CLARK DAVEY: No, I don't think sir, that is what I am saying. And if I can quote you the actual direct quote from a speech I gave recently which has given rise to this debate: I said *The Gazette* will be more reflective in our coverage of the "plurality of culture" which make this city such a fascinating place to live, work, and play. Let me hasten to assure you this does not mean that we are going to abandon our trenchant defence of English language rights and support measures designed to guarantee the survival of essential English language institutions, and it won't shake our belief in progressive Canadian federalism.

CALLER: Those are very fancy words, but your "trenchant" support is a misnomer. You have never exhibited, you or your predecessor, "tenchant support" of the English language.

CLARK DAVEY: Well, there you are quite wrong.

CALLER: "You have contributed to what has happened to the English community here and I think Southam Press is an outside entity, of which you are too, sir, your history is in Toronto and Vancouver.

CLARK DAVEY: I am a Canadian, and I think I have as much right as you, sir, to live in Montreal.

CALLER: You do, you do. But you don't have as much right as I do to represent the English community when you, in an erroneous fashion, contribute to its demise.

MCKENTY: In what sense, sir, do you represent the community? Have you been elected by anybody?

CALLER: Have you?

MCKENTY: No, but I would not say I represent the community.

CALLER: Well I would, because I have lived here for over 60 years.

MCKENTY: Congratulations.

CALLER: What does that mean? Congratulations.

MCKENTY: You say in some sense you represent the Englishspeaking community, and I was asking you, what gives you this title?

CALLER: By being a member of the community for a longer period of time than Mr. Davey. Or imports from Ontario, like you, Mr. McKenty … you do not represent …

MCKENTY: I feel sir, as much a Quebecer and a Montrealer as you do.

CALLER: I know you do. In fact you are NOT.

MCKENTY: So then there are two classes of English.

CALLER: Yes. Those who are imported, and those who are born here.

MCKENTY: We are immigrants, are we?

CALLER: And then take up positions of "representing" the English here, when they simply don't.

10

Building Community

Neil had a cross-cultural following; many of his listeners, like Marie-Anne Coté, were francophone. Among Neil's papers was a letter from Coté, who tuned in to his show in order to perfect her English.

I want to let you know that your radio show was some kind of school, where first, I learned my English, and secondly where I have learned a million things. Your programs have always been so pertinent and so topical, no wonder the lines were always blazing, A lot of my friends have started listening to you because I have encouraged them in order to get better "educated" on a lot of things that were discussed on the blazing lines. Personally, you made my day by informing me on so many things. Your cute quips make me laugh very often. Today's subject is "Is rudeness worse nowadays?" Yes. It all started with the *laisser-aller* on the way people dress, No manners are taught in schools anymore. It will get worse.

Another caller whose life was changed by Neil in a much more personal way was Cathy Robinson.

My first interaction with Neil was in the fall of 1980 when the subject of "Exchange" was "Babies, what's your experience with them?" I picked up the phone and called in. I told Neil I had absolutely no knowledge of babies, but was on my way to the hospital to give birth. My suitcase was packed; I was ready to go. I know that I giggled my way through the conversation. Neil wished me luck and off I went.

Friday mornings there was an opportunity for follow-up calls, when topics which had been discussed all week were hashed over. I phoned to let Neil know that my baby had arrived. But there were complications. Our daughter, Erin, had been born with a cleft lip and palate. However, I did write to Neil to tell him about our girl, and about how many surgeries Erin would have to undergo in order to repair her mouth.

Much to my surprise, I received a letter back from Neil within a week. He just assumed that my husband and I had the necessary strength of spirit that it takes, and would manage through this rather frightening time. His words gave us hope, and his assurance that the Montreal Children's Hospital was a wonderful health care facility gave us confidence. We began our journey through the process of repairing Erin's lip.

As time went on, I would update Neil on Erin's progress. I sent him pictures of my beautiful girl. Life has a way of getting in the way, and years slipped by. Then I was looking at wedding pictures of Erin and her husband, and remembered Neil, and that it had been a while since I had had any contact with him. I sat down, put pen to paper, and filled Neil in on what had transpired, and how we loved our new son-in-law. Neil always replied to my letters and appreciated the pictures and updates. I felt that he was my friend.

Neil touched my life as I am sure he did with many of his friends and listeners. His letters showed compassion and understanding and he encouraged me when I needed encouragement. Watching your child disappear into an operating room, spending hours in the waiting room, can leave one feeling helpless. Having support is vital. I was blessed in that I had a strong connection with my husband and family. But having support from someone outside that circle is important too. The whole process was foreign to us. Today, when I look at my lovely daughter (artist, wife, and mother), I know how lucky I am. That Neil took such an interest in an anonymous caller added to our coping skills.

In 1982 Frank Gallagher nominated Neil as a "Great Montrealer." "He is the host of one of the city's leading talk shows. His ability to handle all types of subjects, and give his audience the time to express their opinions, is always handled in the most gracious manner. His tolerance with senior citizens, who are often very nervous when on the radio, is very heartwarming. Whenever he speaks with children, he never talks down to them and always treats them as equals. May callers keep his lines blazing. May he never run out of fuel."

A Christmas to Remember

Catharine recalls one morning just before Christmas 1983, Neil was having breakfast when he heard that, as a result of corporate funding cuts, Ville Marie Social Services would be unable to provide food baskets for about 4,000 families. Neil immediately decided to do something about it. But he was aware of the risk. What if he raised the issue on "Exchange" and no one called in? Among his first callers were his neighbours, Gail and Gerard Fellerath, who had both served in the Peace Corps. They phoned in to say they would open a drop-off food depot at their store called Folklore 1 on Sherbrooke St. in Westmount. Then the superintendent of an apartment building in the east end said he would do the same. A woman from Rosemere said she would drive people down to that depot. (A third of Neil's listeners at the time were francophone). The appeal snowballed.

Stoph Hallward, a grade school student, volunteered to go door-to-door with a friend to collect canned food. He recalls that Neil's efforts set off a chain reaction throughout the city.

"Neil Mckenty stood out among my parents' friends when I was growing up. It was exciting to know someone I could hear on the radio, but when I think back on it, he never sounded any different hosting his own show than he did challenging my family in friendly banter around the dinner table. His being so so himself was probably what gave me the confidence to call him on his show, once. My friend Roddy and I, who were probably eleven or twelve, decided to join the effort and went door-to-door in our neighbourhood collecting canned food. It was an easy sell and everyone gave generously."

Neil and Catharine drove down to Ville Marie headquarters where they were met by a social worker, tears streaming down her face. "I've never seen anything like it," she said. That Christmas, thanks to Neil, four thousand families were fed.

To everyone's astonishment Neil left CJAD voluntarily in 1985 at the top of his game when he had an estimated 75,000 listeners and his ratings for "Exchange" were at their highest, and in his words, "The lines were still blazing." He quit to write a biography of a Benedictine monk, John Main.

11

Successful Broadcaster
Turns Biographer

**Neil McKenty gave up $90,000 salary
to write about Benedictine monk
Susan Carson
The Gazette, Dec. 31, 1986**

In 1985, 59-year-old Neil McKenty did something that few of us would have the nerve to do. He left a job he enjoyed and did well, which paid him close to $90,000 annually in salary and benefits, in order to stay home and write a biography of a Benedictine monk. Today, 18 months later, McKenty said he misses the excitement of being host of his daily phone-in show "Exchange" which was attracting 75,600 listeners when he resigned. But he has no regrets. "I have not wasted five seconds wondering if I did the right thing. I was still enjoying the program in those last months. But my priorities had shifted so subtly that I wasn't aware of it happening and the consequences of it developed rapidly."

McKenty had already completed the research and some writing of his book on John Main, who founded the Benedictines' first centre for meditation in London, England, and then subsequently opened another in Montreal. But McKenty decided he couldn't complete it without devoting himself full time to the project.

After sounding out several good friends to see how they viewed his decision, and checking with his accountant to make sure he could afford the career change, he turned in his microphone for a full-time job behind a typewriter. It wasn't the first time McKenty had changed his life's course. In 1970, he left the Jesuit order after 26 years, not because he had lost his faith, but because he felt he could make a contribution to the world in some other way Two years later he married and moved to Montreal from Toronto to begin his broadcasting career at the age of 47.

Neil and Catharine McKenty rapidly adapted to their new life in Montreal. The couple took up cross-country skiing and Neil developed a passion for hockey. But still they felt there was something missing from their lives. One day a former Jesuit colleague suggested he contact John Main, a Benedictine monk, who had opened a meditation centre in west end Montreal.

"I found him sitting on the back veranda of a dilapidated old house. We talked about sports and the problems of raising money if your house is falling down," said McKenty in a recent interview in his sunny Westmount living room. "Then he gave me some tapes of his talks on meditation to listen to. Catharine and I found them so fascinating we returned a few months later for meditation lessons and ultimately started our own meditation group. My wife and I still meditate twice daily."

Those tapes changed McKenty's life.

Meditation soon became the lynchpin of his faith. Four years ago (in 1982), Main died of cancer in Montreal at the age of 56. The night he died, his successor asked McKenty to write his biography. McKenty instantly agreed. "There was no question that this was an opportunity for me. Main's permanent contribution to the world was to return a tradition of meditation to Christianity that had been lost for hundreds of years. He built a bridge between Christianity and the eastern religions. I felt a huge responsibility to be fair to Main and to get his teaching right. To get it wrong would have been a kind of sacrilege."

Before Main's death, McKenty knew him as a remarkable teacher of meditation. But afterwards, as he widened his scope of research to England and Ireland, he discovered a man of God whose feet had been firmly placed in the world of man. Main had begun his career as a journalist in London. Then he worked for British Army Intelligence for several years before earning a law degree and joining the British colonial service in Kuala Lumpur. Main wasn't happy with his work, but while there a Hindu swami taught him to meditate using a mantra. A year later he returned to Trinity College in Dublin to teach law, but ultimately became a Benedictine monk. His primary goal was to restore meditation to its former place within the Christian church. It took time. Initially the Benedictines wanted to make use of Main's fine teaching skills. He became assistant headmaster of the order's school in Ealing, England, and later principal of a private school in Washington, D.C., before returning to London to set up a meditation centre.

But gradually he became disillusioned with what he perceived as the lack of prayerfulness or the superficiality of the monastery," McKenty explained. "He decided to develop a foundation of his own where more emphasis could be put on prayer and meditation. He learned that there might be an opportunity to do this in Montreal and ultimately set up a meditation centre with the help of another Benedictine, Fr. Laurence Freeman, who came with him from England."

McKenty's research led to some surprises. The biggest, he said, was the intensity of Main's involvement with a young female medical student in London when he was a professor of law at Trinity College. "I think love was involved on both sides, but there appear to have been too many problems to overcome, including the fact that they lived in two different countries. In the end I think she sublimated her love in her work and he became a Benedictine. However, they never lost touch."

Main and McKenty often had spirited arguments he explained. "I enjoyed his humour, his sense of irony, his clarity of thought and expression. And for me, his Christianity was the real thing. He didn't draw huge crowds. He appealed to ordinary people who found a way of prayer through him that didn't seem artificial. I never once detected a false note."

Neil discovered his Irish roots when he and Catharine made the first of several trips to Ireland in May of 1983 to do research and meet John Main's family and friends of this remarkable man.

Catharine remembers that John Main's sister, Yvonne, welcomed them at her home in Dublin and drove them down to Ballinskelligs in County Kerry. Within days Neil had collected enough material to fill more than one book. To Catharine's surprise, he even managed to scramble part way up the precipitous slopes of Skellig Michael, the rocky island where medieval monks had preserved the ancient Christian tradition of silent meditation which John Main had introduced to Montreal. At the end of their stay they took a fast train from Cork to Belfast where the head of the Free Methodist Church there, Sidney Callaghan, drove them up the coast through the spectacular Glens of Antrim, the McKenty's ancestral home. In Carnalough they saw a row of six houses that Charlie McKenty built more than a century earlier. Charlie McKenty would carry most of his materials on the front of his bicycle. Once in a while he would stop work to do a little jig for the sheer joy of it. You can still see the graceful plaster moulding Charlie placed on the outside wall of the local pub and on the inside wall of the Catholic Church.

Neil was so engrossed in the ongoing challenge of capturing on paper the life and times of his Irish subject that it was then that he decided to leave CJAD at the peak of his broadcast career. On their next and much longer visit to Ireland in 2003, Neil decided to find out something about his mother's family, the Sheas. His search took them through the lovely village of Adair, with its thatched cottages still intact, to a remote valley. Later, he wrote about the experience for the Irish publication, *Nuacht* (Sept 2006).

How the Sheas arrived in Canada:

You may think that the name Coolcappa refers to one of those drinks of iced coffee we enjoy in the summer. In fact, it is a small village on the border of Limerick where my Irish ancestors, the Sheas set out for the new world in June 1825. Coolcappa comes from the Gaelic, *Cull Cheapach*, which means "corner of the village plots." This spring, my wife Catharine and I spent a morning there mucking around the parish graveyard in the warm rain looking for names on weathered gravestones that might give us a clue about who was left behind. We also chatted with the lovely woman who keeps the grocery store/post office as clean as whistle and filled with laughter from her wonderful Irish stories.

Of course the Sheas, also known as the O'Sheas, are one of those storied Irish families that came from a long lineage working its way back through hill and dale, war and peace, to the early bogs and mists of ancient Ireland.

Here we catch up with them in the early nineteenth century when the Sheas had long been farmers in County Limerick. Unfortunately, the economic situation in the early 1820s was grim. In 1821 the potato crop failed, causing great distress among the lower classes who subsided mainly on a diet of potatoes and buttermilk. To deal with the situation, the British government decided to underwrite the cost of sending carefully selected families from the south of Ireland to Upper Canada, giving them free land (70 acres), and supplying them with tools and a year's supply of rations. At one stroke, this policy would reduce suffering in Ireland and provide more men for the militia in Upper Canada, still nervous after the War of 1812. To get this scheme off the ground, the British government contacted the Attorney-General of Upper Canada, Sir John Robinson, who turned to his elder brother, the Hon. Peter Robinson, at that time the Member of Parliament for York. Quickly, Peter Robinson travelled to Ireland and began lining up volunteers to leave for the new world. Although only a limited number could be accommodated, many thousands applied, sick of their poverty and lack of prospects at home. And this despite the fact that Robinson was peppered with questions about the presence of bears, wolves, and marauding Indians.

Best Book of 1987

Mary McAleese, who was to become the President of the Republic of Ireland, was taken with Neil's book In the Stillness Dancing: The Journey of John Main. Writing in The Irish Catholic, McAleese described it as the best book she had read in 1987.

A chance conversation with an academic colleague introduced me for the first time to Dom John Main – Benedictine monk, lawyer, lecturer, Irishman, and spiritual guide. I became especially interested in him on discovering that like me he had lectured in the School of Law in Trinity College. At a time in my own life when I felt the deepest need for developing and growing in my prayer life, I found John Main's simple and unadorned introduction to Christian meditation exciting and effective. His biography, with the magical title *In The Stillness Dancing: The Life of Father John Main* taken from a poem by T.S. Eliot, is an intriguing insight into this man of many contradictions all unified in his love of Church and Christ. This is not one of those impenetrably sycophantic biographies of the saints. It is a frank account of a difficult and perhaps even to some an unlikeable man – an identifiably human, human being, whose quest for Jesus shines and shines through an often controversial life. Through him I learnt again that we do not have to like to love, to understand before we say we love. His taped talks on stillness and meditation have helped me through more than one traffic jam and more than one dark night. In his own words "The New Testament summons each one of us to live not on the surface or in the shallows but from our own depth of spiritual experience."

He is undoubtedly a great teacher on that journey from surface to self.

Christmas Letter, 1987

To say that Catharine and I haven't written a holiday letter often is a gross exaggeration. We've never written one. But those from some of our friends have given us so much pleasure we thought we'd give it a shot. Of course the result will be erratic – like our cross-country skiing in the Laurentians – but we have fun doing that, and we're hoping you'll have some fun reading this.

The past year has been indeed remarkable. It began in January when my second book, *In the Stillness Dancing*, was published in London, England. To back track a moment. I had been doing public affairs broadcasting since 1972 ... during my last ten years, I hosted what became a popular phone-in program, "Exchange." So why did I resign? That brings me back to the book. In the fall of 1977 two Benedictine monks, John Main and Laurence Freeman, arrived from London to begin a meditation centre in Montreal. Because of a chance remark, I met Dom John Main in 1979 – a tall, impressive man with a sparkling Irish wit rooted in his own origins in County Kerry. Gradually we learned more about his life: Jesuit educated, British Intelligence Service, a student and later a professor of law at Trinity College, Dublin, civil servant in Malaya, barrister, Benedictine monk. In Malaya John Main met a charismatic Hindu near Kuala Lumpur who led him by a circuitous route to a Christian form of meditation going back to the 4th century and beyond – a form of meditation that induces deep interior silence through concentrating on a prayer word, or mantra. It was this form of Christian meditation that John Main came to Montreal to develop and teach.

His teaching was intense, but short. In December 1982, John Main died of cancer at the age of 56. The night of his death his close associate and friend, Dom Laurence, asked me if I would be interested in writing John Main's biography. I accepted immediately ... during the next couple of years, Catharine and I spent as much time on research as we could. This involved intense working trips to Dublin, London, and Washington, where John Main spent most of his adult life. (Catharine tried to convince me that we should go to Malaya, but Il y a une limite.) Publicizing John Main's biography was a joint enterprise.

In this effort, Catharine and I were helped by many friends. Sister Gertrude McLaughlin advised us on the book from the beginning. John and Clare Hallward lived through every phase of the book with us. Clare is an excellent editor which means she not only improved the text but she also never took my tantrums seriously. John's enthusiasm carried us through the difficult periods inherent in writing any book. All of us had fun at the book launchings in Montreal, especially at the Double Hook with Judy Mappin, the Anglican Diocesan Book Room with Jack Sheppard, and the United Church book store with Mary Beth Moriarity. I was able to talk about the biography on radio, and it was especially gratifying to return to my old program, "Exchange," where my successor, Joe Cannon, asked me to stay for a second hour.

In Montreal, the festivities climaxed with a reception hosted by the Prior, Laurence Freeman, at the Benedictine Abbey on Pine Ave. About this time, Catharine and I flew to Syracuse, New York, to give a seminar on Christian meditation – it is not as difficult as you might think. All the important parts are in silence.

While all this was going on we still managed to get to the Laurentians for several week-ends of cross-country skiing. Catharine and I are not great skiers, but we enjoy the outdoors, the lovely Laurentian mountains, and the camaraderie around the blazing fireplace. Joining the winter instead of fighting it seems to make it shorter. It seemed short indeed this year because in the spring we were off on a trip to which we had both long looked forward. The first stop was Dublin. The highlight of our stay was a reception at Trinity College (founded in 1591) to launch the biography. Main had been a student and a law professor at this cottage and lived in a lovely suite of Georgian rooms where his sister Yvonne helped him entertain students, some from his beloved Malaya. We stayed in a house near the sea where James Joyce once walked and wrote. We flew to London for ten days, where we explored Churchill's cabinet war rooms. After seeing a couple of plays, and dancing up a storm at a lively Italian restaurant, and making my usual pilgrimage to Speaker's

Corner in Hyde Park, Catharine flew off to Germany and I flew back to Montreal making vague plans to write a biography of Catharine's grandfather, R.J. Fleming, four-time Mayor of Toronto. These plans were rudely interrupted by a telephone call from the executive producer at Montreal's only commercial English language television station, CFCF-TV.

Boulevardier Nick Auf der Maur at the launch of Neil's book, *In the Stillness Dancing*, 1986.

McKenty had always wanted to do television, to find out whether he could be "any damn good at it." In 1987, CFCF, (now CTV) offered him a chance to do a local television show which its producer, Don McGowan, envisioned as "a poor man's Larry King" (King was a highly rated U.S. broadcaster who went from a show on Mutual Radio to CNN television.) Like McKenty, King was direct and non-confrontational. McGowan recalls that the one thing Neil did not want to do was a radio talk show on television.

Don McGowan Remembers

Initially, I was concerned about Neil adjusting to television following his many years behind a microphone in the less intimidating confines of a radio station. He approached his new challenge with vigour, working with a large production team, including the producer director, Daniel Freedman, a floor manager, cameramen, lighting director, make-up artists and production assistants. Neil was a true original, and we enjoyed having him as part of the CF family, his booming yet friendly voice bellowing through the hallways. Of course Neil had to wear make-up. In the basement grotto where the performers were made to look a few years younger, our make-up artist, Miss Elly, talked and joked as she applied the base and powder to Neil's face. I don't think he enjoyed that part of the television game. (It might have been a Jesuit thing.) Although he adapted well, he was often frustrated because he had less time to develop and expand the subject material with his guests and with the viewers who called in.

I remember two editions of "McKenty Live" that were particularly provocative. One show was on the subject of "Swapping Mates" and the other on "The Joys of Nudism." Neil did not remove his very expensive Warren K. Cook suit for either program, for which I am thankful to this day.

The "on-camera talent" at CFCF were expected to make public appearances. On a hot July evening a promotional event was staged aboard a ship docked at Victoria Pier. Neil drew a large crowd because of his huge radio audience at CJAD. He was erudite, witty, and kindhearted. I was proud to have lured Neil from downtown to our television studios on Ogilvy Avenue!

One day Neil announced he was going to buy a car. He was a terrible driver. I suggested he warn the motoring public first. Typically, Neil did his research and decided to buy a pre-owned Mercedes Benz because it was a safe automobile. I told Neil it was a good choice because Mr. Bronfman drove a Mercedes, but perhaps he might want something more modest like a Chevrolet or a Volkswagen.

Unlike me, Neil was always in touch with a higher being. He bought the Mercedes.

12

Neil McKenty's Back, and this Time He's Live on TV

Mike Boone, *The Gazette*, May 29, 1987

One of Montreal's most popular radio hot-line hosts will try his hand at TV, on CFCF-12. McKenty left broadcasting to finish a book he had been writing, *In the Stillness Dancing: The Journey of John Main.* After touring to publicize the book, McKenty settled down in his Westmount home to contemplate his next project, a biography of R.J. Fleming, a mayor of Toronto in the late 1880s (and incidentally his wife's grandfather). The book was never written.

The broadcaster turned author did not think about a return to the airwaves. "I wasn't waiting for the phone to ring," McKenty says, "But the ring came, and it was not a ring you get very often in a lifetime." McKenty live on television won't consist entirely of its host talking to people on the phone. The show will be flexible, with the capability of gearing itself toward the day's hot news story. McKenty does not want to be the host of a radio show on TV. The inspiration for the show is the television version of "Larry King Live," a phone-in program. There are lots of tight close-ups on King and his guests, Don McGowan says Channel 12 viewers will see the face that McKenty's 75,000 radio listeners never saw. "We know we don't have Robert Redford here," McGowan says, "but we're not going to get the putty knife out for Neil's crow feet. His face has character, credibility – all the reasons we want McKenty."

Dr. Ruth and Neil.

McGowan is buying a proven commodity. Through 14 years at CJAD, eight as host of "Exchange," McKenty built a solid reputation in Montreal. Whether or not you agreed with McKenty's opinions, you had to credit the former Jesuit priest with integrity and intelligence at a time when integrity and intelligence were rare on phone-in shows. The hot-line genre was popularized by a succession of fire-breathing demagogues such as Joe Pyne and Pat Burns. McKenty was different, both on and off the air.

Neil interviewed some remarkable guests: Dr. Ruth, the sexologist who was so tiny she had to sit on a telephone directory; Louis Riesman, Canada's chief negotiator for the North American Free Trade Agreement, with whom Neil had a ferocious argument two days before the 1984 federal election. Former Quebec Premier René Lévesque was one of Neil's guests in October 1987. During the exchange, Neil asked Lévesque if he believed in God and in an afterlife. Lévesque said "Yes" to both questions. Lévesque stated that, in spite of the church's checquered reputation, it was where he found, and continued to find, spiritual nourishment. Two weeks later, René Lévesque was dead.
But Neil's most memorable television guest wasn't a celebrity, but an ex-convict, Gilles Thibault.

Thibault was one example of a trend on the show that became more pronounced in the 1990s. McKenty was becoming less interested in experts and celebrities and was becoming more intrigued by the first-hand experiences of people who had grown through pain: recovering alcoholics, battered women, victims of child abuse, ex-convicts, and in how they managed to not only survive but overcome the painful ordeals which they had to cope with in their lives. The idea was to inspire others, "still in the dark tunnel," and persuade them not to despair.

Over the years in radio and television, I interviewed many movers and shakers, but the most memorable was Gilles Thibault. I doubt the name Gilles Thibault means anything to you. Nor to me either. Until one wintry morning early in 1990, when Gilles was a guest on my television show. I walked onto the set, and Gilles was waiting for me, a short, spry, balding man of 59, dressed sharply in a grey suit with a blue shirt and red tie. He was Québecois, but his English was impeccable. He had just written a book, *J'ai passé 42 ans en prison.*

How, I wondered, could a man who had spent 42 of his 59 years in jail, (mostly in maximum security penitentiaries at hard labour, when he wasn't isolated in the hole,) survive. We spent much of the program trying to answer that question. When he was about 12, his mother, who was a prostitute, sent him to a boarding school in Rigaud run by the Christian Brothers. One day, when he learned that his mother, who was paying for his education, had died, he was refused permission to attend the funeral. So he stole a bicycle and went anyway. He was apprehended for theft and sent to a detention centre.

In 1945 he was sent to Bordeaux Prison for robbery. In prison he was assigned to a detail which required him to cut down the bodies of men who had been hanged ("when other boys were learning to love"). Canada still had capital punishment. In all he served 42 years in prison for armed robberies, theft, and for trying to escape. He wasn't very good at escaping, he joked. He was not a violent person, but prison is a violent place. He was beaten, sexually abused, and lashed by authorities. He went 20 years without a single visitor. He spent a lot of time in isolation, and told me he thought about suicide.

How did Gilles turn his life around? He had no easy answer, but there were elements of an explanation. One night in his cell, trembling with hopelessness, he fell to his knees and asked God—if there is a God—to help him. At that point Gilles Thibault seems to have had a genuine spiritual experience which changed his life. After reading his memoir, I expected to meet an angry and bitter person, resentful that he had been shortchanged by life. Not at all. He knew who he was and what he had been. And he knew the difference. There was no self pity. He regretted what he had done. Now he was getting on with life. He was a whole person in a way many people never achieve. In a quiet, confident voice he answered callers, many of them ex-cons or prisoners on parole. I was especially pleased when a senior officer with the Montreal police force called to congratulate Gilles on what he had made of his life. Gilles admitted he had been a criminal, he had owed society a debt, and he had paid it. Now he was happy and comfortable in his skin. He had been married for a month and was bubbling with wonder and joy at being with his wife, and with being alive. How did Gilles Thibault do it? He had no easy answers. But after he prayed, he learned that a judge who had the power to have him declared a habitual criminal, refused to allow the authorities to lock Thibault up and throw away the keys. Some indomitable spark of his own spirit refused to be snuffed out, no matter how dark the tunnel nor how distant the light at its end.

In my book, Gilles Thibault is no longer a criminal or a victim or a problem for society. I wish him well. In my book he's a winner. I will never forget him.

What worked on radio didn't work on television. For one thing Neil had little sartorial sense. No matter what he wore on television he seemed rather unkempt. For another, the warmth that he projected on radio seemed calculated on television. He was a pro, but was never truly relaxed in the glare of the camera's eye. The commercials especially threw him and interrupted the rhythms of his conversations. He was easily distracted by the floor crew moving around the small studio. Once, while Neil was interviewing a guest, a cameraman tossed a roll of duct tape across the studio to the floor manager who caught it effortlessly. The cameras were live but the toss was out of range, over the shot. When the show ended Neil lambasted the crew. He didn't have the cool McLuhanesque demeanor that television demanded. The week the show made its debut, the Gazette's television critic, Mike Boone, was less than impressed.

McKenty's Talent Wasted on Television

"McKenty Live" continues the Canadian television tradition of ascribing life to dead programs. Neil McKenty, former host of CJAD's "Exchange" phone-in, has brought his considerable intelligence and talent for discussion to television, where both qualities are wasted. Viewers might recall another gifted radio personality who tried his luck at TV. Peter Gzowski, arguably the best broadcaster in Canada, was host of a CBC television show called "90 Minutes Live." Unfortunately for Gzowski, who deserved better, and for the CBC, which could ill afford an embarrassing failure, the lifelessness of "90 Minutes Live" doomed the late-night talk show to scathing critical notices and indifferent viewer response. Ten years after the debut of Gzowski's television program (and eight and a half years after its cancellation), Channel 12 is trying to turn a radio host into a TV star.

"McKenty Live" is, in essence, a television version of "Exchange." McKenty begins the 30-minute program by suggesting questions that callers might wish to ask the program's guest. After a brief introductory chat, McKenty and his interview subject go to the phone lines. I missed the debut of "McKenty Live" but caught yesterday morning's program, which featured comedian Dave Broadfoot. The telecast was marred by a technical foul up: for several agonizing minutes, between the opening chat and the first commercial break, none of the incoming calls were audible to McKenty, Broadfoot, or the audience at home.

These things happen on new shows.

The bugs were ironed out during the ads. Then McKenty cheerfully announced that "the lines are blazing" (his favorite comment on "Exchange") and he and Broadfoot, one of the stars of the Royal Canadian Air Farce, discussed comedy with several Montrealers.

"McKenty Live" screens incoming phone calls to ensure that the babbling bozos who are the bane of Montreal talk radio do not get through to sabotage the television program. Callers on "McKenty Live" are people with questions that are lucid and reasonably interesting. But the quality of calls doesn't matter.

You could have Pierre Trudeau on the blower talking to Brian Mulroney and "McKenty Live" would still be a radio program trying to pass as television.

The phone-in format works on radio because the spoken word commands attention on radio. Radio is an intimate medium. The listener is involved in very intense one-to-one communication with an effective radio announcer.

Television is different. It is difficult to concentrate on what is coming out of the speaker box when you're watching television. The eye takes over and the ear gears down, which explains why the TV research and development people invented colour, slow motion, and freeze frame long before they got around to stereo. It may be unfair to judge a low-budget morning program by the criteria one might apply to prime time. Perhaps people who watch the tube at 10 a.m. aren't looking to be jolted out of their seats by rapid-fire pacing and high-gloss production values.

Neil McKenty has a lot of fans in Montreal. Channel 12 hired him to cash in on the announcer's popularity and ability – and also, it must be said, to fill 30 minutes of air time with a locally produced show that doesn't cost much and can be enjoyed by people whose picture tubes have blown.

But let's get the title right. Just call it "McKenty."

The Gazette, Sept. 30, 1987

Tony Kondaks, *Author and blogger.*

Neil and I hardly agreed on anything. Yet we both respected and acted with civility towards each other. Actually, he was much more civil and patient towards me than I was to him; he earned my respect by not taking the bait, so to speak, every opportunity I found to "push his buttons" on a particular issue.

As a result, he taught me that it was more effective to make my point with honey rather than with vinegar.

So I attempted to always maintain a proper tone in my correspondence with him on this forum. I mostly succeeded but not always; Neil, however, always did. I can't remember him ever crossing the line with me and I can assure you I gave him more than one tit-for-tat opportunity. I don't know why I was drawn to this forum on such a regular basis. Perhaps it was the open-ended question format that Neil employed. Or the short, succinct way he had of expressing and introducing the topic of the day that got all of us regulars chiming in. I had originally found the site as a result of a Google search on "Bill 101", found an entry here on the topic, registered my opinion (you all know I have lots of those!) got hooked, and never left.

13

A Change of Focus

Neil put television behind him in 1990 to focus on his writing. He also worked with the Quebec Canada Committee doing his part to keep the country together. He told the Vancouver Sun's Tom Barrett, that in spite of perceptions on the West Coast, Quebec is a pretty good place to live. Barrett profiled Neil in a newspaper story:

After 20 years in public affairs radio and television, McKenty doesn't look like a troublemaker. His grey hair, grey steel-rimmed glasses, and grey suit present a solid, respectable, and very Canadian image. But for people who don't like to see French on their cornflakes boxes and wish that Quebec would just shut up and leave, his message is less than welcome. "Despite our problems in Quebec, with language particularly, it is still a good place to live. We are there, we are staying there, and we want people to know it is our home and it's a good place to live." The Quebec Canada Committee took out a full page advertisement in 35 English-language Canadian newspapers. "This is a big country with a big heart," the ad said. "With generosity of spirit we can build it anew." Response to the ad was two to one in favour, which McKenty says is a good ratio. "The response from francophones has been almost uniformly positive, saying "My heavens the English community is saying something positive about Quebec." As politicians lurch towards a new constitution and author Mordecai Richler burns up the lecture circuit attacking francophone Quebec, McKenty and other members of his committee are on the road "trying to build a bridge" between French and English.

Neil and Catharine continued their charitable endeavours, Neil joined the board of Nazareth House in order to establish the first AIDS hospice in Montreal, and both of them worked at the Benedictine priory giving talks on Christian meditation. Working with the AIDS Hospice, gave Neil a deeper understanding of gays and the stigma attached to AIDS.

Should Gays Be Celibate? "Pit Stop" 2008

A most unusual story is now developing in England. It concerns the famous 19th century churchman, John Henry Cardinal Newman, one of England's greatest prose stylists. Newman, who wrote "Lead Kindly Light" and "The Dream of Gerontius," was first an Anglican priest, then a Roman Catholic convert who became a prince of the church. What has caused the uproar in the gay community in England, and among many Catholics, is the Vatican's decision to exhume Cardinal Newman's body and move it to a shrine in Birmingham in anticipation of his beatification. So what's the problem? The problem is that Newman explicitly ordered in his will that he wished to be buried in the same grave as his long-time friend, Father Ambrose St. John. And so he has been for more than a century. A new poll shows that 80 per cent of the readers of the *Church Times* oppose the Vatican's decision, and want the body to remain where it is.

Most outraged is the gay community. The gay rights activist Peter Tatchell says the Vatican's decision to move Cardinal Newman's remains is an act of grave robbery and religious desecration. It violates Newman's repeated wish to be buried for eternity with his life-long companion and partner, Ambrose St. John. "They have been together in the same tomb for more than

100 years, and the Vatican wishes to disturb their peace to cover up the fact that Cardinal Newman loved a man. It is a shameful, dishonourable betrayal of Newman by the gay-hating Catholic Church."

However, a respected Catholic spokesman, Austen Ivereigh, takes a different view. "I don't think anyone disputes that Cardinal Newman deeply loved Ambrose St. John. He did say after St. John died that his grief was comparable to a husband losing a wife, but he did not mean that their relationship was a gay marriage. It is simply wrong to read back from today's categories into the Victorian age when these very intense, passionate but *totally celibate relationships in Oxford among the Anglo Catholic community were very common.* (Italics are mine). Lurking beneath the surface here is the question: was John Henry Newman gay and what does that mean in the predominately male context in which he spent most of his life?

There is considerable evidence that Newman was homosexual. There is not a scintilla of evidence that he lived out his homosexuality in a sexual way. The Catholic haters and the skeptics will say this is impossible. But is it? Should we deny the possibility of a deep and tender love between males without any hint of a sexual connotation? We are all familiar with profound relationships and non-eroticised love between males and females, such as between mothers and daughters and fathers and sons. An even better example is the relationship between a happily married man and a close female friend who is not his wife. "I have certainly experienced that myself" One of Newman's successors, the late Basil Cardinal Hume, once wrote. "To love another, whether of the same sex, or of a different sex, is to have entered into the area of the richest human experience."

Amen to that.

Meanwhile, the battle of words about the Newman affair gets more vitriolic. And the Catholic Church is under growing pressure to abandon its "homophobic" exhumation and reburial of one of its most famous cardinals, in defiance of his specific wish to lie for eternity next to the man he loved.

14

Depression Strikes

After John Main died in 1982, Neil and Catharine become more and more involved in the Priory on Pine Avenue. Main was succeeded by Dom Laurence Freeman, a bright, engaging articulate young man who tried to carry on the tradition of the Priory as a place where people came to learn Christian meditation. Underneath, problems were simmering, exacerbated by personality conflicts. The Priory eventually closed in 1991. It was turned over to the Roman Catholic Archdiocese of Montreal. This put an end to a fairly close-knit group, although Neil was named chairman of a lay committee which continued to meet and continue their sessions.

By March, 1994, Neil increasingly felt that he was a failure, and "plunged into a bottomless shaft of gloom." He was determined to kill himself. He decided to commit suicide by jumping in front of a train in the Metro. He wrote about it in The Inside Story.

I knew it would be messy for me and for those who survived me, especially Catharine. But I was no longer thinking of others. My inner being was like an inkwell overflowing with nothing but black thoughts of nothing but myself. I had never before felt so helpless and hopeless, so sunk in a curious state of perturbed paralysis. I wanted to sink even deeper into the soft nothingness of death.

Suddenly, a flash like heat lightening lit up the oppressive gloom in my head. Momentarily, I glimpsed the flames of hell and damnation flickering the way the Catholic Church had painted them for me as a little boy. I could see the forbidden sex of my Jesuit years and taste the warming gurgle of alcohol melting the ice in my soul. Then the moment of clarity vanished. The clouds rolled in and the tapes in my head – the suicide tapes – began playing again.

I had long since given up the idea of shooting myself or death by drowning. The tape now playing in my head was about a plunge onto the tracks of the Montreal Metro. Slowly and laboriously, I found a pencil and a piece of paper and wrote a suicide note: "Dearest Catharine, I think you will be better without me, Love Neil." Then I folded the paper, my own obituary notice, and placed it carefully on the floor just inside the front door. I shuffled along to a bar on Sherbrooke St. I thought it would be easier if I had a drink, although I hadn't had one in years. The world around me, the people, the cars, seemed unreal, as if I was looking into a green-coloured fish tank. I sat at the bar for a few minutes, but I didn't order a drink.

Then I trudged to the Vendôme Metro station, walked down the steps into the metro, went out on the apron, and sat on a bench about twenty feet from the tracks. I stared glassily as about half a dozen trains rolled by.

Then I got up and went back home. I think I was then, for just a moment, in a moment of calm – the eye of the storm. The physical activity of walking in the fresh cold air had briefly stilled the suicide tapes and given me back just enough momentum to take a positive step. Back home I dialed the number of my young friend, Chris, with whom I had breakfast occasionally. I don't know what the outcome would have been had he not answered. But he did, and invited me to join him for supper at a neighbourhood restaurant. I agreed, went to the front door and tore up the suicide note.

While picking at supper I described to Chris as well as I could what a hell hole I had been in all day. Then with a kind of groan and with a strangled voice that came from deep inside of me, I said to him, "I just want to be real." Only six words, but they distilled a lifetime. I could no longer endure the split of feeling one way about myself, but needing others to feel another way. I could no longer summon the energy to bear the mask to maintain the charade, no longer wanted to be a performer. I desperately wanted to be real and needed help to make the journey.

In 1997 Neil published his autobiography. The book is forthright, pulls no punches, and speaks for itself. The Gazette's religion columnist **Harvey Shepherd** *summed up the narrative in this review on April 19, 1997.*

Struggling with 'snarling dogs': Former broadcaster Neil McKenty charts his spiritual journey in excellent autobiography

The title of Neil McKenty's new autobiography, *The Inside Story*, might for some readers evoke his lengthy career in journalism, mostly electronic. But while there are some interesting recollections of broadcasting experiences, any readers hoping for scandalous revelations about, say, the inner workings of radio station CJAD, will be disappointed. I cannot imagine, however, anyone else being disappointed by this wonderful book. As you read it, you realize what profoundly religious and spiritual themes can be evoked by the *The Inside Story*. Published by Shoreline Press of Ste. Anne de Bellevue and selling at $18.95 in paperback, the book has the subtitle *Journey of a Former Jesuit Priest and Talk-Show Host Towards Self-discovery*.

Not the least of its virtues is what a workmanlike piece of writing it is. It is worthy of a communications pro who has spent many of his 72 years in the media, and is known to many Montrealers as a former radio talk-show host and TV host. I found the book a real page-turner, right from the March 1994 incident with which he opens the book. And what a jolt that incident gave me! I first became more than just vaguely aware of McKenty's existence in 1986, through my work as a religion reporter when his biography of the late Dom John Main was published.

Main founded the Benedictine Priory of Montreal, precursor of what continues today as the Unitas ecumenical centre for spirituality and as Christian Meditation groups. Subsequently, I had some contact with McKenty and his wife, Catharine, as leaders of the Christian Meditation movement and, later, leading supporters of Unitas. I admired and, to a degree, envied them as regular practitioners of a spiritual discipline that I presumed had brought them a certain enlightenment and serenity. I still suspect, by the way, that I was right.

Imagine my surprise to learn on the first page of his autobiography that in 1994, about seven years after I became aware of McKenty, the Christian meditator, he was in the grips of a depression and was seriously contemplating suicide. And, to top it off, he was thinking of doing the deed by jumping in front of a Metro train! My surprise is something of a symbol for me of a central theme in the book. To a great degree, The Inside Story is about the contradictions between the way people and institutions may appear on the outside and what you may discover about them as you get to know them better. Such contrasts appear again and again: in McKenty's strait-laced but quietly alcoholic father; in the fire-and-brimstone teachings of the Catholic church in which he was raised in Ontario; in the Jesuit order, where he spent 25 years; in the Benedictine Priory; and in John Main's successor as head of the Priory, Laurence Freeman. But above all, such contrasts racked McKenty himself, especially as a Jesuit priest who, among other things, drank too much and managed to begin a love affair within a year of his ordination, continuing it for more than a decade. He reports that a contrast between a successful exterior and a seething interior also marred his successful broadcasting career and marriage.

Although the distinction between the inner and the outer is central to the book, McKenty never seeks to titillate with gratuitous gossip. Nor is there any mawkish pretension to tell all emotionally. *The Inside Story* is written with great restraint. The reader is well aware that, in summing up such a rich life in 160 readable pages, the author must have left out much more than he put in.

McKenty makes relatively little attempt to convey to us the flavour of either the spiritual highs or the emotional lows of his career as he relates the facts surrounding them. Both are largely beyond the power of language to describe. There is little description of the spiritual benefits he has derived from Christian Meditation, which he obviously counts among the spiritual treasures of his life. And in describing the ravages of his recurring depression, he often refers to it as "the snarling dogs," and pretty well lets it go at that. At one point, however, discussing his depression between 1992 and 1994 – "almost two years of a horror I could never have dreamed existed" – he does write that "we have no language to discuss (clinical depression) adequately," but then proceeds to make some attempt at doing so for about a page. It was "the emotional turbulence of all the past years – the anger, the anxiety, the fear, the loneliness, the shame and resentment – like a clogged toilet backing up and overflowing into my bloodstream and my brain with all the stinking and poisonous detritus of a lifetime's disease. "I say the brain, and no doubt depression is a malady of the brain. But depression, as felt and experienced, is a sickness of the spirit, a cancer metastasizing from the soul."

McKenty feels this is pretty well behind him. For details of how that came about, I refer you to the book. But he gives a large part of the credit to Jim Reed, a man influenced by the 12-step approach of Alcoholics Anonymous and other self-help groups. (Interestingly, drinking was no longer McKenty's problem. He had quit years earlier.)

McKenty's restraint shows up to especially good advantage when he discusses the rift that developed in the Christian Meditation community in Montreal in the years after Main's death. The split was hell for McKenty and played an important part in triggering the worst period of his depression. Even writing about it must have been pretty excruciating. But he has achieved a remarkable sureness of touch. McKenty's situation was particularly difficult because he had few, if any, direct problems with Freeman and had been close to him.

No doubt McKenty makes some points that others would put differently. But McKenty strives to avoid raking over old coals any more than is necessary.

Describing the worst period of his depression, McKenty writes, "I felt my life had been a waste and a failure. As I looked back over the years in Hastings (Ont., his home town), in the Jesuits and in the media, there was no sliver of satisfaction, only the overwhelming sensation of unreality and hypocrisy. I felt a knot of self-hatred and loathing." McKenty is describing the pathology of his depression here, not summarizing the way he feels about his life now. But these comments are also a strong statement of a central problem with which he has struggled through his life.

As they read of how he struggled, I suspect many readers will, as McKenty hopes, "be helped on their own journey towards wholeness."

"People who suffer from depression will learn through this book's testimony that even when everything seems to be failing, hope should prevail. –Pablo Cervantes, Director of the Mood Disorders Clinic, Montreal General Hospital.

15

Jim Reed's Roadmap for Recovery
by Neil McKenty

Little did I know that a new found friend, Jim Reed a former sergeant major and CEO of two shipping companies would guide me on a new journey and save my life. Sitting at his kitchen table I said in desperation that I needed help and I needed it right now. "All right," said Jim, "This is what we are going to do." Then as though he was firing a machine gun he laid out a program of activity that made my head swim – which is precisely what he intended. He wanted to change the tapes.

First, I was to come to his apartment on foot, six nights a week, at seven o'clock, for a discussion. Every evening before I came I was to sit down at my desk and write out a detailed agenda of my next day's activities. I was to fix a reasonable time for getting up in the morning and stick to it. I was to do at least one hour of physical exercise each day – preferably brisk walking. I was to watch for interesting films, to get me out of myself. I was to sign up for a weekend with a group of Jim's friends because their serenity and laughter might well be contagious. And I was to plant some kind of garden in my back yard so I could get some real earth on my hands and stop and smell the roses. As I walked home after that first meeting I felt a twinge, almost imperceptible but still real, – a twinge of hope.

So I set my alarm clock for the morning and to make doubly sure I would hit the deck running I arranged to have breakfast with a friend in a nearby restaurant. I also became involved with Benedict Labre House for Montreal's street people.

And every evening after supper I set off for Jim's place on foot. Often we discussed incidents that had happened that very day, incidents which now seem inconsequential and picayune, but in fact revealed to Jim and ultimately to me patterns of behavior and attitude. How did I feel when Catharine asked me to get a loaf of bread? Did I usually open the car door for her? What triggered my last outburst of anger and did I see that it was a control issue? Presently I realized this was the key. Jim equated attitude change with personality change. In a way Jim was helping me change the lenses through which I had viewed the world and this change was rooted in and related to a spiritual experience. Because ultimately that is what the depression itself was, a fundamental spiritual experience.

In biblical terms, I had to lose my life in order to find it. The depression had driven me to my knees. Jim told me to get on the floor each night before going to bed and each morning after rising and put the day in the hands of God, whether I believed in God or not.

As this program of activities, exercises, and discussion continues through the spring and early summer of 1994, slowly, imperceptibly at first, my depression, like a fog on the landscape, began to lift. And I began to see and enjoy experiences – simple things I had not for two years – a boat trip around the harbour, a sour cream doughnut, a genuine spontaneous laugh from deep inside. This was the best because I had not laughed for two years. In a moment of profound crisis when I had admitted to myself

I was helpless I reached out and there was someone there. I gave up on the obsessive drive to control. From being fragmented and torn apart inside, I started to feel more whole. For the first time in my life the ball was hitting the glove, the arrow the target. I felt I was fitting in, connecting in a way I had never had before, with myself, with other people and with my understanding of God.

> *There were two Neils. The one who needed an image of himself and the other who loathed the image that others had of him. He was a super, super guy, but he was distracted by the pain of living.* Jim Reed

16

Christmas Letter, 1998
by Neil McKenty

I had never heard the sound before. It was like guns firing in the night. In fact it was the sound of trees cracking and crashing in the January ice storm, the most spectacular and devastating storm to lash our city and our province. At the height of the storm I walked at night along Sherbrooke St. – a ribbon of light with army lorries lumbering by and bumper to bumper traffic crawling along like sluggish caterpillars. Just to the north the city was enveloped in inky blackness, while all over the province power lines collapsed and the lights went out, sometimes for weeks. Dreadful as this experience was for many, there was a sense of awesome, almost exhilarating beauty about the storm, like sheet lightening illuminating the sky or the sun glittering on ice.

Not that Catharine or I were inconvenienced much. Our only casualty was the loss of one of our three tall apple trees in our back garden. It fell in a shower of sparks and ice pellets across the property of our two neighbours. Were they upset? On the contrary. They got our their power saws, cut the tree into little pieces and arranged for most of it to be carted away. I guess that's the image most of us will remember, how the ice storm, paradoxically, warmed our hearts and gave our neighbourhood, our city, and indeed the whole province a sense of community that never had been felt before.

I experienced this in a tangible way when I spent a few hours every day at a shelter in Victoria Hall where many of the temporary homeless remembered me from my days in radio. There were no strangers in the ice storm.

It was a smooth transition from the ice storm to cross-country skiing at the Laurentian Lodge. We usually go up every weekend in the winter, often in time for a ski before lunch on Friday and stay through until Sunday, skiing on the old railroad tracks, sitting before the roaring fire, reading, chatting, and eating. Catharine and I also continue our close association with our good friend, Steve Sims, who has helped many young people, especially with their addiction problems. Twice a month at Steve's place, I co-ordinate an Exchange, a spiritual discussion group, where we tackle everything from gay spirituality to palliative care, and whether religion has a future. We also spent a retreat with the Indian Jesuit, Tony De Souza.

We interrupted the retreat so I could give a commencement address to the 1998 graduation class at Loyola High School. It was a singular honour for me to return to a Jesuit school where some of my former colleagues in the order were still active. I urged the graduates to begin to draw their own maps for the journey ahead of them, but I tried to convey a light touch with the advice of Yogi Berra, that when you come to a fork in the road, take it.

In May, I wrote my first monthly column, *Pit Stop*, for the *Senior Times*. Our remarkable autumn, warm clear and dry, was broken not by snow, but by the decisive victory of the Parti Québécois in the general election. We have been around this track so many times, I do not detect any of the anxiety that was provoked by the elections of previous PQ governments. Our new Premier, Lucien Bouchard, is a powerful leader, acutely tuned to the French-Canadian psyche, but I seriously doubt that even he can achieve the "winning conditions," for another referendum on sovereignty. As we head into the new year, I can't resist blowing my own horn. To our amazement and our gratification, my memoir, *The Inside Story*, has been chosen by a survey of Globe and Mail readers as their favourite book of the year. Later we learned that a major book distributor in the U.S. had taken the book.

Looking back at the experience of six decades or more, I am reminded of what T.S. Eliot said,

> "We shall not cease from exploration and the end of all our exploring will be to arrive where we started, and know the place for the first time." Blessings on your journey.

Neil began writing Pit Stop, a monthly column for the Senior Times which proved to be popular with readers.

I was enjoying a winter holiday in Palm Springs, California, when it was announced that Sargent Shriver had died. In the early 1970's I met Shriver, who was married to President John F. Kennedy's sister Eunice. Mr. Shriver was the founding director of the Peace Corps, the signature success of Kennedy's New Frontier. He also directed Lyndon Johnson's War on Poverty, founded Head Start, created the Jobs Corps and Legal Services for the Poor. He served as President of the Special Olympics which was founded by his wife. Writing in the New York Times, Bob Herbert said that "Mr. Shriver affected more people in a positive way than any American since Franklin Delano Roosevelt."

When I first met Shriver in 1971, he struck me as an enormously enthusiastic and energetic man. I met him to discuss an award the Kennedys were making to Jean Vanier, the son of a former Governor-General of Canada. Mr. Vanier was being honoured for his work with the mentally challenged. My boss at the time, the Toronto philanthropist and sportsman Harry Red Foster, thought it would be appropriate if our prime minister, Pierre Trudeau, wrote a short statement which would be read at the awards ceremony in Washington, D.C. I called Mr. Trudeau's office and he readily agreed. There was, however, one condition. His statement would have to be in both English and in French, and must be read that way. Mr. Shriver readily agreed, and said he would find someone who would handle the French. At the event, however, someone dropped the ball. To my exasperation, the statement was not delivered in French. I expressed my anger to Mr. Shriver. He was as upset as I was, and apologized profusely.

As this was playing out, we were negotiating with Eunice Shriver to have Canada play a larger role in the Special Olympics. We had a Canadian Special Olympics at Exhibition Park in Toronto and we had been invited to join the Kennedys for the first international Special Olympics in Chicago.

One of the most successful elements of our own Olympics was floor hockey. We had convinced the National Hockey League to get behind the project and we were eager to have Mrs. Shriver accept floor hockey into the American Special Olympics. To that end I had several meetings with Mrs. Shriver in Washington. What a tough lady she turned out to be – tough in the sense that she knew what she wanted and used any means to get what she wanted. Smart, too. I was not the only person who thought that if Mrs. Shriver had been born later, she might well have become the first female president of the United States. She questioned me carefully about the suitability of floor hockey for the Special Olympics. Then she bought our proposal, lock, stock and barrel.

I am writing this in Palm Springs, where I have talked to a lot of people about the Obama presidency. People are either for him or against him. There is no middle ground. As one of the naysayers put it, "My husband had a job under George Bush, he lost it under Obama." My own view is unchanged. Obama will win a second term fairly easily. I mean, who is likely to beat him? Sarah Palin?

Golf was an important part of Neil's life. In one of his Christmas letters he wrote about playing his final game of golf for the year on November 23, 1998, with the temperature at an unseasonable 14 degrees C. That year he played golf in Georgia, Vermont, Maine,

Ontario, and at his own course in Montreal, Meadowbrook. All told, he was on Meadowbrook 125 times, for more than 1,200 holes of golf, never using an electric cart, except when he played at Big Canoe, in Jasper, Georgia, where a cart is mandatory. Because he played so frequently, he was often asked whether his game had improved. The answer was "not much," but he kept working away at his swing. He enjoyed the game, got a lot of good exercise, and met golfers in their 90s who had a positive outlook on life. Neil was content on the fairways.

McKenty's Two-Rule Golf School

"Keep it simple, stupid!" Imagine if those four words were applied to the golf swing. It would revolutionize the game. Since I left my television show 12 years ago, I have been trying to master the golf swing. Let's face it, the swing has more rules than a monastery: bend your elbows, incline your knees, swivel your hips, flex your ankle, equalize your weight, overlap your fingers, and address the ball. In trying to keep all this straight, the danger is you begin to hallucinate. You wake up in the middle of the night yelling "Fore" and you haven't even hit the ball.

Is there any way to get a handle on this jumble, any way to "keep it simple, stupid?" As a matter of fact I think there is. It came to me the other day at Meadowbrook where I try to play several days a week. Of course all golfers have their own theories about the golf swing. For what it is worth, here's mine. It seems to me you can reduce all these rules and regulations to two. One relates to the head, the other to the feet. Keep it down and don't move. Simple, but not easy. How can I tell if I've moved my head during my golf swing? Simple again. The ball dribbles along the fairway like water dribbling from a garden hose that's lost its pressure. Whereas if I keep my head steady the ball arcs gracefully into the air every single time. So it's not your elbows or your wrists or your knees. It's the head, stupid. And I would argue that if you don't move your head, you are halfway to a good golf game. So do I keep my head still. Not every time. But often enough to keep me coming back.

After the head there's the feet. What about them? Move them. The exact opposite of what you do with the head. To be more precise, you don't exactly move the feet. What you do is move your weight from one foot to the other, and in the process, both feet move in different ways. So how exactly does this work?

When I address the ball I try to keep my weight evenly on both feet. Then on my back swing I try to move most of my weight from my front foot to my back foot. And on my follow through I try to move the weight from my back foot to my front foot. I don't often do it correctly but I try. In going from front to back, the front foot moves slightly. In going from back to front, the rear foot pivots so that at the end of the swing you are standing on your rear toes facing the target. So, it's true that both feet move in different ways. But the purpose of the whole exercise is to move or transfer the weight. Again, simple, but not easy. The fact is that most of the time I can't manage it.

How can I tell if I have moved my feet (transferred my weight) correctly? I can tell every time. If I haven't, the swing has no power and the ball won't go far. It's like a gun that has lost its charge. The bullet has no velocity.

So, to resume. If I move my feet, I get distance. If I don't move my head, I get height. If you have both height and distance you are a long way toward an enjoyable golf game. Just for the record, I have this other idiosyncrasy that makes my game still more enjoyable. I don't count. So instead of logging a triple bogey from the last hole, each hole for me is a fresh start. And believe me, I don't need to count to tell whether my swing is working or not.

If you are a golfer you may disagree with my diagnosis of the golf swing. But you have got to admit, it's simple. And if I could find a partner, I think we could make some money. We'd start the Two Rule Golf School. "Don't move your head, move your feet." We couldn't lose, could we?

17

Skiing Legends

Early days of skiing fondly recalled: Laurentian Lodge members going downhill since 1924
Alan Hustak, *The Gazette*, February 3, 2001

The Laurentian Lodge Club in Prévost is nothing at all like the rented condos that abound in the fake corporate Alpine villages up north. Perched in the shadow of the Big Hill, 60 kilometres northwest of Montreal, it offers great skiing within a short distance of several resorts in the area. It is one of those rare and rustic places that grew out of youthful camaraderie and into tradition.

Veteran Montreal broadcaster Neil McKenty and his wife, Catharine, have belonged to the club for 27 years. Together, they have written *Skiing Legends and the Laurentian Lodge Club*, a social and anecdotal history of an institution that's high on the social slopes of Montreal.

The club began in the winter of 1922 when the 34 original members, all of them men, shelled out $15 each to join. It wasn't formally registered until March 13, 1924. Then, on September 29, 1929, the club bought a farmhouse for $8,000 to accommodate its members and the Lodge Club has occupied the building ever since.

Its wraparound verandah was originally painted in hideous shades of red and green, and it was once described as the ugliest house in the province. The lodge wasn't easily accessible, the furnishings were second-hand, and the accommodations were rudimentary.

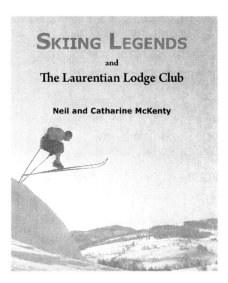

"It had no special cachet, the beds squeaked and the showers leaked," the authors write. "Why not join a prestigious club, where you sank into the leather chairs and leaned back while the uniformed barman bought you a drink? Precisely because these men sensed there was still something of the frontier spirit in the mountains. They didn't want to lean back and go slack. They still sought challenges and they found them skiing in the Laurentians."

The McKentys might be right about the challenge, but the suggestion that the club had no special cachet is disingenuous. It was written up in the *New Yorker* as early as 1929. As skiing became an increasingly popular pastime during the Depression, it was one of the few places in the Laurentians where you could indulge in it for a weekend.

Members have included Percy Douglas, the first president of the Canadian Amateur Ski Association, Herman (Jackrabbit) Johannsen, the legendary outdoorsman who lived until he was 115, Dr. Wilder Penfield, founder of the Montreal Neurological Institute, and Douglas McCurdy, the first person in Canada to fly an airplane.

From its inception the club was also popular with Americans, including the patrician Boston Cabots, the New York Chryslers, and Dr. Irving Langmuir, who won the Nobel Prize for chemistry in 1932. Philadelphia millionaire Joe Ryan was a guest even before he had the idea of turning Mont Tremblant into a ski resort. The Laurentian Lodge Club was also the first in North America to install a rope tow. In 1930, McGill student Alex Foster hoisted an old car on blocks, removed one of the back wheels, and used it to drive a pulley that drove a rope tow up the big hill. To commemorate the inventor, one of the trails toward Saint-Sauveur is known as Foster's Run.

The club is one of the last anglo bastions in the province – members still refer to Prévost as Shawbridge, even though the name was changed in 1974. You have to look hard for francophones among its members, although Major General Edouard de Bellefeuille Panet was president in 1939. Panet apparently resigned because he couldn't bring his Irish setter into the lodge.

Today a membership will set you back $500 a year, and the number of members is limited to 90.

Skiing Legends and the Laurentian Lodge Club is thoroughly researched and includes splendid photographs that provide an affectionate snapshot of the past.

The book is a welcome chapter to the regional history of the Laurentians, one that might have easily been overlooked. And the longer the lodge itself stands, the more important it becomes in telling the story of the development of recreational skiing in this country.

18

The Other Key

A short story Neil wrote for his writing class developed into the only novel he wrote, The Other Key. The book, an Inspector Julian Main murder mystery was published in 2003. It appeared on the best-seller list for a couple of weeks in December, largely as the result of word-of-mouth. Neil told the Westmount Examiner's Dorothy McLeod how the book came to be.

"I was persuaded by a friend to take a writing course at Thomas More Institute. The idea was that over two to three months we would write a short story. I decided to do a detective story. It just bloomed up. We did exercises each week, very imaginative exercises, like describing where your hero lives so that readers will understand what sort of person he is. The short story came to 10,000 words. People said they would like to know my characters better. So, with a considerable amount of trepidation – not having written fiction since high school – I started a novel. All I knew was the ending. I had the beginning of an idea about the protagonist, a detective. I set myself a rigid schedule. I wrote from nine until noon, then had lunch, and a few rounds of golf, then wrote from four to six. It was getting engrossing." Although the novel takes place in Montreal, he added scenes from England and Ireland, which he had visited on an earlier research project.

When he had written 50,000 words he had a few copies bound and sent them to friends, neighbours and fellow students to read.

They were enthusiastic about the book, but found some problems. In the novel he describes his hero getting stuck on ice in his Saab. "One reader pointed out that a Saab would never behave like that because it is a front wheel drive, and I had described the behaviour of a rear wheel drive car. I had a guy drinking a martini and three paragraphs later it was a manhattan."

A novel, he discovered, needed to be researched. So he phoned Detective Steve Roberts of the Homicide Division of the Montreal Police Department. "He read it in two sittings, he liked it, but my crime scenes were all wrong. He generously made a whole bunch of notes." Next Neil felt he needed to get into the morgue and watch an autopsy and he spent several hours there taking notes. Despite the corrections and rewrites, he describes the process as being "a lot of fun, creating something out of nothing."

Would he do it again? "I don't think so."

On the other hand he says, "I'm getting a great deal of 'Is this the first in a series?' There might be another one to emerge."

19

Merry Band of Bloggers

In 2008 Neil started a blog which took off with a bang and quickly attracted what he described as his "merry band of bloggers." The one which attracted the most hits was "Is Religion a Hoax?"

IS RELIGION A HOAX?

Bill Maher is one of my favourite comedians. He is funny and he is caustic. Both these traits are on grand display in Maher's documentary film, *Religulous*, in which he visits religious communities around the world from a trucker's chapel in North Carolina to the Vatican and concludes that religion has done more harm than good.

Maher's own religious background is ambiguous. He was born to a Jewish mother and a Catholic father: "I used to go to confession, but I would bring a lawyer."

Maher sees organized religion as one of the world's great evils, responsible for wars, crusades, the oppression of minorities, "the keeping of women in beekeeper suits," burning witches, exorcisms, honour killings, and sex with children: "Did I leave anything out?"

He expects protest and he's used to it. For instance, when Pope Benedict visited the United States in April, Maher said that if he had been the head of a nationwide chain of day care centers that had covered up so much child abuse, the Holy Father would not have been given a parade, he would have been arrested.

Maher acknowledges that religious groups have been an effective organizing tool for charity work, soup kitchens, feeding the poor and missionaries – but claims all of this could have been accomplished without "the bells and whistles of religion."

Maher says the point of *Religulous* is to make people laugh and then realize with a start that there may be some truth in what he is saying.

Maher also hopes his documentary will start a real debate about the efficacy of religion: "This is the last taboo. For the longest time people have not even broached this subject. You can't even talk about a person's faith. Why don't we examine a person's faith or ask the more basic question that I ask in the film, "Why is faith good? Why is it good to stop thinking?"

Maher rejects the notion that his film is an attack on extremist religious groups only: Have you seen the nonsense and the destructive nature (of the Bible)? – because it's as integral to religion as the Constitution is to the United States.

"If you believe in a talking snake and you believe that the world is 5,000 years old [cue Sarah Palin] and you believe you're drinking the blood of a 2,000-year-old space God on Sunday, ipso facto, you're a rube."

Maher's polemic reminded me of a conversation I had this summer in Maine about religion with a couple who had just turned forty. The woman had been brought up a devout Catholic in Ireland, the man an Anglican in Montreal. I would think they are now atheists.

Neither of them could understand how so many people could go on believing that the man Jesus now resided, living and breathing, in a paper-thin slice of bread. Where other people saw a sacrament, they saw the Eucharist as a male power grab to control millions of credulous people over the ages.

Do you think they're onto something? Is Bill Maher onto something?

Is religion a hoax?

Neil's last column appeared in the Senior Times May, 2012. In it he challenged the Church to take a more nuanced approach to its teachings about sexuality. In it he wrote that he did not believe in a God who would condemn anyone to death for unrepented moments of sexual pleasure.

Church risks moral irrelevancy in rejecting homosexuality.

Few issues have so bedeviled the Catholic Church as those of gender and human sexuality. Yet the Vatican shows no sign of changing its teachings in these areas. It is reported that since the time of Pope John Paul II, all candidates being considered for bishop must be sound on these issues: they must be opposed to female priests, artificial contraception, and same-sex marriage. It is not surprising then, that few bishops ever step out of line on these matters. Those who do risk their ecclesiastical careers. Retired Australian bishop Geoffrey Robinson is an exception. Robinson recently spoke in Baltimore at a symposium on Catholicism and homosexuality. He called for a new study for everything to do with sexuality, a kind of study which he predicted "would have a profound influence on church teaching concerning all sexual relationships, both heterosexual and homosexual. If church teaching on homosexuality is ever to change, the basic teaching governing all sex acts must change," he said. Robinson argued that the church's moral appraisal of same sex unions would change dramatically if it were to evaluate its traditional approach to all human sexuality.

While the church's emphasis on the profound significance of sex is correct, its natural law approach to sexual morality and its interpretation of ancient scriptural passages on homosexual and other sexual activity are in need of correction, the bishop argued. Robinson began his talk with three basic premises: there is no possibility of change in the teaching of the Catholic Church on the subject of homosexual acts unless and until there is a change in its teaching on heterosexual acts; there is a serious need for change in the church's teaching on human sexuality, and if and when this change occurs, it will inevitably have its effect on the teaching of homosexual acts. "If the starting point is that every single sexual act must be both unitive (loving) and procreative, then there is no possibility of approval of homosexual acts. Robinson then went on to suggest that a more nuanced reading of divine commandments in scripture and of Jesus' teachings would lead to a different moral conclusion, starting with a change in teaching that every sexual act or thought which falls outside a loving conjugal act open to procreation is a mortal sin because it is a direct offense against God himself and his divine plan. "For centuries the church has taught that every sexual sin is a mortal sin. That teaching may no longer be proclaimed as loud today as it was before, but it was proclaimed by many popes, has never been retracted, and has affected countless numbers of people. The teaching fostered a belief in an incredibly angry God, a God who would condemn a person to an eternity in hell for a single unrepented moment of deliberate sexual pleasure arising from sexual desire. I simply do not believe in such a God. Indeed, I positively reject such a God." I expect that many Catholics, priests and bishops would agree with Robinson, but dare not say so publicly because they fear retaliation from Rome.

An influential American Journal, *The National Catholic Reporter* is solidly behind Robinson's call for a new sexual ethic. "We wholeheartedly second the invitation by Bishop Robinson for a thorough and honest re-examination of the church's teaching on sexuality."

Robinson's invitation is a gentle but elegant plea that offers hope for Catholics who want to stop the church's headlong plunge into irrelevancy as a moral voice on our culture. Robinson's take on sexuality – that it deserved deeper consideration than the narrow rule-bound approach that has evolved in fundamentalist Christian circles – takes us to the very radical approach Jesus himself took towards human relationships. Indeed, it is likely that a large number of lay Catholics in Canada and the United States agree with Bishop Robinson on the church's need to reform its teaching on sexuality. But many more voices – both lay and clergy – will need to say so and be heard before such reform becomes a reality.

Dr. Anne Hallward
Host of award-winning Safe Space Radio on WMPG Portland Maine. "I called Neil my radio dad. He listened to more than 70 of my radio shows. He always gave me frank and helpful advice about how to frame the questions and focus the topic. I call my show 'A Live Forum for Courageous Conversations.'"

20

Drawing Your Own Map
by Neil McKenty

Once I was hosting a radio phone-in program when the question was, "How do you get on with your mate driving in the car?" Calls were a riot. Most of the callers, especially the women, recalled incidents when their husband got lost. The reaction was invariably the same. First the husband denied he was lost; the he refused to stop the car and ask for directions; finally in a fit of pique, he angrily declined to look at the map.

That program got me thinking about maps. Of course, if you're lost it's stupid not to look at a map and figure out where you are. But suppose you didn't have a map. Or something worse, you had the wrong map. Imagine, for instance, you live in Montreal and you are motoring to Boston. Everything's fine until you arrive in Beantown. Then the whole trip begins to unravel. You can't find your hotel; you can't even find the name of the street your hotel is on. You pore over your map. You can't find a single name or reference point that makes any sense. You continue to drive around aimlessly, bewildered, growing more anxious and angry by the minute, totally frustrated. Finally, you spot a policeman. You stop and show him your map.

He looks at you quizzically and says it's no wonder you're lost. You've been driving frantically around Boston. But you're trying to follow a map of Detroit. You have the wrong map.

Isn't that how many people go through life following the wrong map? And if that's the case (and experience suggests it is) then is it any wonder that so many of us are anxious, bewildered, angry, frustrated and ultimately lost? Is it surprising that we experience a chronic inner dis-ease, that we are not comfortable in our skin and that we expend enormous energy trying to disguise this condition from the outside world?

Of course, we are now talking about an interior map, a map that relates to the landscape of our own psyche, the topography of our innermost soul. So where did we get this defective, inaccurate map that has led us down so many blind alleys, cul-de-sacs and roads that went nowhere? In my case the map I followed for many years goes back to my boyhood. What's wrong with that? Nothing, except the map was drawn by other people. From as long as I can remember I was trying to live up to the expectations of other people: my parents, my priest, my teachers and, to some extent, the community in which I lived.

Trying to live up to the expectations of others never works because (in your own mind at least) whatever you do, however much you succeed, it is never enough. The bar is continually being raised. What this leads to is not a genuine sense of accomplishment but an oppressive sense of failure. We can never do enough. And it's not far from feeling that we are failures to feeling that we are unlikeable. Not just that others don't like us but, fundamentally, we don't like ourselves.

This is a recipe for inner dis-ease. And disguising that dis-ease from others and even from ourselves becomes our objective. We desperately try to project an image that all is well, we can manage, we are a success (as we well may be), we have a great social life and scads of friends. And if these external accomplishments do not anaesthetize the inner pain for long (which they don't) well some of us try a quicker method, chemicals of some sort. A double martini or a snort of coke will deaden our dis-ease a lot faster than making a successful speech or writing an acclaimed article. But whether its alcohol or drugs or success we are all, in a sense, addicts, trying to fill a spiritual hole with a material reality.

Which brings us back to maps. At the core of the problem is an instinctive sense that we are not being true to ourselves, that we are not living out of our own natural bent, not, in the words of Joseph Campbell, "following our bliss". Instead our lives are still governed by external expectations, by maps drawn by other people. To be specific, think of the tortuous journey of a man who really wants to be a writer but instead has become a priest. Or a woman who wants to be an artist and finds herself doing a doctorate in bioethics because that's what she thought her father, an eminent doctor, wanted her to do. I think the word hypocrite is relevant here, not in a moral sense but in the root from the Greek, hypocrite meaning "actor". It's a dreadful burden to go through life being an actor, following the wrong map.

How does one turn this situation around? How does a person develop his or her own map for the journey? Not easily. Not by any more external band-aids or success stories. The outer journey (with the wrong map) must be replaced by the inner journey using the map that enables us to become the person God intended us to be.

But how do we move from outer accomplishments (which like drugs require stronger doses) to an interior journey that deals with our dis-ease in a fundamental and permanent manner?

This is a movement from disliking ourselves to liking ourselves, in my opinion the most fundamental spiritual transformation imaginable. I think the first step is a total revulsion at the unreality of the way we have been living expressed perhaps in a cry from our inner depths, "I just want to be real". My own experience is that a crisis of some sort may be required to get us to this existential honesty, something along the lines described by the American Jungian therapist, James Hollis, as the "swamplands of the soul". These include loss, depression, grief, loneliness and betrayal.

Some of us, at any rate, must hit what AA calls an "emotional bottom" wherein we realize we are powerless, that our lives have become unmanageable and we must reach out for help. It is in this "bottom" that I believe we take the first decisive step in beginning to draw our own map. It is a marvellous paradox that when we become vulnerable we also become able to grow from the inside.

In this sense, God does indeed write straight with crooked lines. Or as the Canadian therapist, Marian Woodman, puts it, "God comes through the wound."

How do you know when you are living out of your own map? Let me suggest a few simple test, so simple you may think them jejune. Believe me they're not consider the following :

1) A friend calls you on the telephone to invite you to a party. You tell the friend you'll get back to her. The reason for your delay is not to consult your agenda. The reason is that you don't really want to commit yourself until you're sure another, more interesting invitation doesn't turn up. You are not living out of your own map. The relevant advise is " Move in a straight line. " Only those who habitually live out of their own map are mature enough not to continually hedge their bets but to move in a straight line.

2) Another friend calls on you to take on a project of some kind. You hesitantly say yes, not because the project really interests you (and you already have too many projects on your plate) but because you don't want to displease your friend.

Trying to live up to the expectations of others never works because (in your own mind at least) whatever you do, however much you succeed, it is never enough. The bar is continually being raised. What this leads to is not a genuine sense of accomplishment but an oppressive sense of failure. We can never do enough. And it's not far from feeling that we are failures to feeling that we are unlikeable. Not just that others don't like us but, fundamentally, we don't like ourselves.

This is a recipe for inner dis-ease. And disguising that dis-ease from others and even from ourselves becomes our objective. We desperately try to project an image that all is well, we can manage, we are a success (as we well may be), we have a great social life and scads of friends. And if these external accomplishments do not anaesthetize the inner pain for long (which they don't) well some of us try a quicker method, chemicals of some sort. A double martini or a snort of coke will deaden our dis-ease a lot faster than making a successful speech or writing an acclaimed article. But whether its alcohol or drugs or success we are all, in a sense, addicts, trying to fill a spiritual hole with a material reality.

You are not living out of your own map. Only those who do feel really comfortable saying "no" when "no" is the nature of the response. How and why a person says "no" is a fairly accurate test of whether that person is living out of his or her map.

3) You do something in public, e.g. a talk, a presentation, an article. There is very little or no reaction from others. You are inordinately discomfited by this lack of response. You are not living out of your own map. To change the image, you are still dancing to the music played by others.

There are many other examples of not living according to your own map and I expect you can come up with many of your own.

Drawing your own maps is not a decision, an act of will. It is a process which requires awareness, demands patience but is truly liberating, and blessings on your journey.

Neil McKenty

21

Journey's End

During the 2008 U.S., Presidential election campaign primaries, Neil travelled to Unity, N.H. to see Barack Obama and Hillary Clinton campaign. He didn't live to see Obama re-elected. In 2012 he and Catharine went on a Caribbean Cruise. Four months after they returned Neil died on May 12, 2012. He was 87. His producer Daniel Freedman delivered a tribute at the funeral.

Some people make a difference in the world. Neil McKenty was one of those people. Though he often led a troubled life himself, Neil ended up making the world a better place. That's because he touched many lives. Mine was one of them. Like so many others I grew up listening to Neil on CJAD. Nobody did a call-in show like Neil. His gift went beyond putting a fierce intellect to work in building bridges at a time when so many others were trying to blow them up. Neil actually listened.

He could get politicians to actually think on the air and say something unexpected and newsworthy. And he could get callers to open up about the most intimate details of their lives. And all because he listened. And because he cared. Life's rich pageant unfolds in unexpected ways.

One day in 1987 I was surprised to find myself in my boss's office at CFCF (now CTV) Television, meeting Neil for the first time. The meeting was to discuss the possibility of reviving Neil's radio program for television. The boss was Don McGowan, who in his inimitable style saw fit to begin the meeting with the question, "So Father McKenty, do you still consider yourself a good Catholic?" As my mouth dropped open, Neil remained unfazed. "Yes," he instantly replied, "I do consider myself a good Catholic … in my own way." Mr. McGowan was reduced to silence. The first and only time I saw that happen.

The program went ahead and I became the producer. Mr. McGowan, in his largesse, made the grandiose gesture of sending a limousine to pick Neil up each morning. But since this is Montreal, and not Hollywood, the so called limousine turned out to be a very big, but a very old and noisy Cadillac. And since I lived near Neil, this ridiculous vehicle also stopped to pick me up. On the first morning Neil said to me, "This really is a bit much." He was embarrassed. I later learned that Neil had once turned down a suite at a hotel. The suite was to have been his reward for speaking at a conference. But Neil was embarrassed by the fuss. He asked for a regular room instead.

That was Neil. He hated pretense. And he hated hypocrisy. I saw him show the same respect for a make-up artist, stagehand or waitress that he showed for a professor or a prime minister.

Neil's idea of a good time was dinner and dancing with his wife, Catharine at the Rib and Reef Restaurant, not exactly the Starlight Lounge at the Waldorf Astoria. Neil once told me "I've made many mistakes in my life, but I got one thing right. I married Catharine. I'm the luckiest guy alive."

I long ago concluded Neil was one of the most complicated and interesting men who ever lived. For much of his life, Neil wrestled with demons. But through it all, and behind the somewhat formidable exterior, Neil had a great gift for friendship. Neil also had a great capacity for mentorship. I worked on Neil's program with two exceptional colleagues, Joan Takefman and

Wendy Helfenbaum. We called our team Three Jews and a Jesuit. You never knew what to expect from Neil. He could be funny, he could be demanding, he could be endearing, and Lord knows, he could be exasperating, all in the same conversation.

For a time, Neil shared a tiny, glassed-in office with Dick Irvin (the station's sports director). But Neil seemed to have bionic ears, an uncanny ability to overhear what we were saying and correct many of our errors of logic from afar, in that booming voice so familiar to everyone. But we always knew that Neil cared. Neil cared about a lot of things. He cared about the truth. He cared about humanity. He cared about his church, with whom he was so often at odds.

On one occasion, an author who had written a book critical of the Vatican was a guest. To my astonishment, Neil took her to task. His point was that somewhere along the road of criticizing the church, she had taken a detour and had invented her own religion. Neil thought that was cheating.

So life with Neil was never dull. He ate ice cream on the air with one of the founders of Ben and Jerry's with great gusto, but very little elegance. Once, when asked to comment on Pope John Paul II's visit to Montreal, Neil uttered the immortal words: "I am having an ecclesiastical orgasm." Who else could have gotten away with that?

On one occasion, we experienced every producer's nightmare: catastrophic technical failure while live on air. Neil was left alone on a single camera with no capability of talking to guests or to callers. Most broadcasters would have melted under the pressure. Not Neil. Talking and arguing was never a problem for him. If he had to argue with himself, well that made it all the more fun. So Neil ad-libbed for almost 15 minutes, making such perfect sense that viewers thought it had all been planned.

One thing stands out above all else. Above all, Neil was always interested in justice. I am sure Neil is already in Heaven. And I suspect he is already fighting to make it a better place, arguing that too many people are excluded, and that that's unfair.

After all, Neil always fought the good fight here on earth. Why would he stop now?

Harold Thuringer, *a former Liberal Member of the Quebec National Assembly and a director of the St. Mary's Hospital Foundation, who served as a volunteer in India, Nepal and with the First Nations in Canada was a friend of Neil's for more than 20 years.*

He had an amazing ability to bring up current topics and have people explore, debate and discuss them, issues related to the Catholic Church, to spirituality, politics, literature, history, and current events. He adeptly ran many social groups, hosted radio and television programs that addressed these issues, and was often invited to moderate community forums. Politics, both Canadian and American, were his cup of tea. He was a liberal, and was a particularl fan of President Obama and the Democratic Party. He would also tune in regularly to FOX News and become particularly agitated by Glenn Beck and Rush Limbaugh. Neil took an active role in the Meech Lake debate, travelling across Canada with other Quebec leaders to support it and to lend his leadership and his wisdom.

Neil's history of growing up in a small Ontario town during the Depression, followed by his years as a Jesuit, seemed to mark him profoundly, especially when it came to spending money on himself. We once stayed at the Chateau Frontenac, where Neil refused to pay $15 for a hamburger in the hotel restaurant and made his way across the street to a café where the prices were more in line with his upbringing. He was generous to charities and to individuals who continue to benefit from his largesse, always making sure that the cause was efficient and consistent with the basic human values and rights that he held so dear. Aside from the regular Exchange meetings, we would always get together two or three times a month for breakfast, sharing our concerns, fears, and joys. I always came away feeling I learned something or discovered a new idea. One of the most intriguing questions that he would ask is "Why do you want to live?" We talked about this over a period of two or three years, and it proved to be interesting how our responses to the question evolved and changed over time.

We also shared the occasional golf game at Meadowbrook, along with other duffers and more proficient players. Neil was the only golf partner I have ever played with who didn't count his strokes. As a result, he was more relaxed about the game after a number of bogies and mulligans, all of which was entertaining and left me in good spirits enjoying the outdoors and our friendship. After Neil died, I gratefully inherited some of his golf balls, shoes, shirt and a blazer. But I could never fill Neil's shoes. I considered him a close friend, and in spite of our different backgrounds, skills, and intellects, he allowed me to be myself and always seemed interested in and tolerant of my many unwashed ideas and convictions. I think of him often and miss him greatly.

*Songwriter and veteran radio talk-show host, **Vin Smith**, who is heard on the "Midnight Bookworm" Family of Radio Shows in the United States, discovered Neil's blog and became an enthusiastic contributor.*

One day I found an e-mail from Neil's blog in my in-box. I checked it out. I was shocked at how I agreed with Neil's entire mindset. I shouldn't have been surprised – Neil turned out to be as progressive as I am. The problem seems to be, especially in the United States, that in spite of the right wing's claim otherwise, most commentators and their bosses are dead-brained conservatives. I suppose that's logical. Most major publishing and broadcast syndicates have always been owned by money men – and they are almost always conservative ideologues. That holds true from William Randolph Hearst to Rupert Murdoch.

But Neil spoke a different language. Don't get me wrong. Before the Neocons and then the Tea Party mental midgets hijacked the American Republican Party, there were actually savvy conservatives in many places. The late Paul Harvey was one of them. I was a big admirer of Mr. Harvey. Once, when I attended one of his speeches, Harvey said, "Jesus asked us to be fishers of men … instead we have become keepers of aquariums, robbing each other's fish bowls."

Without question, Neil McKenty was the Canadian Paul Harvey. Or perhaps Paul Harvey was the American Neil McKenty. I didn't always agree with Paul Harvey's politics, but I always agreed with Neil McKenty's. It takes a big mind to be a progressive in a nitpicking conservative English-speaking western culture, where the watchword is always, "What have you done for me lately?"

Neil McKenty often came out with well-turned phrases that often caught my attention. But, more frequently, he would write very simple truths that we often basically overlook. Like this bit of information from *In The Stillness Dancing: The Journey of John Main.*

"The great illusion that most of us are caught in is that we are the centre of the world and everything revolves around us … this is a very easy illusion to fall into because in the opening consciousness of life it seems that we are understanding the external world from our own centre. And we seem to be monitoring the outside world from an interior control centre. And so it seems the world is revolving around us. Then logically we begin to try to control that world, to dominate it, and to put it at our service. This is the way to alienation, to loneliness, to anxiety because it is fundamentally unreal."

It would be incredibly hard to try to think of another writer who influenced me more. You may remember that the American country singer, Willie Nelson, sings that his heroes have always been cowboys. My heroes have always been teachers. I make my living as an editor, among other things. Polyfaceted am I, and I thank my mentors for that. A good many tidbits came my way from Neil McKenty. The wisdom from his agile mind – especially his searing questions – made us think. I would have taken any course that Neil decided to teach, even if it was underwater basket weaving.

John McKenty, *author, retired high school principal, Neil's nephew*
For three young boys – Mike and Bob and myself – growing up in Kingston, Ontario, our uncle Neil could be an imposing and at times intimidating figure – the deep voice, the wide ranging intellect, the stellar reputation as a teacher and as a writer. We first knew our uncle as a priest. When he came to stay with us in Kingston he would stay at Regiopolis College, the Jesuit High School. Should a Sunday morning occur during his stay he'd say Mass in the small chapel at the school. When that happened our mom and dad would gather us up and off we would go to the chapel. Because we were altar boys Uncle Neil expected us to serve his Mass. The problem was that the McKenty boys were not all that good at being altar servers. In spite of the fact that we would often flub our Latin, Uncle Neil would tell us we were the best altar boys he ever had. My brother Mike reminded me that in the McKenty household Uncle Neil took precedence over Santa Claus because should he visit at Christmas there would be no presents opened until we had been to the chapel and back. As the years went by Neil continued to live the stuff of legend in the McKenty family – his work with the Special Olympics, his marriage to the most wonderful Catharine, and his growing reputation as a writer and as a radio and television broadcaster. I recall one time my wife, Zeta, and I went to visit Catharine and Neil. They took us down to enjoy the night life in Old Montreal. It was wonderful, a club with musicians and magicians and when it was all over Neil hailed a taxi and instructed the driver, "66 Somerville Ave," from the back of the cab. The cabbie said, "Hey, I know you, you're McKenty Live!" It is one thing to be a reporter in a small town in Hastings where everyone knows your name, but it is quite something else to be recognized in a city of three million.

Like his brother Stafford before him and, indeed, like the McKenty boys who followed him, Neil has had his battle with demons. I believe it was those very struggles that allowed Neil to understand and empathize so fully with the struggles of those around him. We are proud of the life our uncle lived and grateful for the legacy he leaves us.

Robert Fleming, *co-founder of PACE magazine, Los Angeles*

Neil was a man who loved to throw the cat among the pigeons. The best thing that ever happened to the Fleming family took place when Neil married Catharine. Neil conquered the hearts of a very Protestant family from Toronto. "Keep the family together," had been the final words our Aunt Evelyn, and for the past twenty years Neil became that keeper. A dedicated golfer, Neil instituted the Fleming Classic Gold Golf weekend each fall, bringing together a group of cousins who have known each other since we were nine or ten. Apart from golf and good food, Neil prodded us to debate great issues. On one occasion a rather heated religious discussion focused on the life of Jesus. Our host and chef later confessed that he had listened in from the kitchen. Fascinated, he went off and bought the book Neil had been reviewing. Blown by the winds of change, Neil and Catharine together became a transforming force wherever they went. Neil was a joy.

Barbara Moser, *Publisher, Senior Times.*

Neil was a master of argument and always gave us the big picture. He was most concerned by the failure of his own Roman Catholic Church to adapt its core teachings to evolving ethical values. He championed those politicians who displayed his own passion for the rights of the marginalized. He had no patience for hypocrites or double dealers. That is why readers of the Senior Times awaited his monthly Pit Stop column, as did his editors, myself included. I was proud to have Neil as one of ours. He raised the bar and set the standard for engaging and thought-provoking journalism. Over the years, Neil's writings helped shape the Senior Times, always reflecting our values and our concerns as a newspaper. We will miss him dearly.

Paul Belyea

Neil McKenty was just a name to me when I was a child. He was a fragment of my father's conversation, a name on a book, a distant face looming out of my dimly remembered past. My father, William Belyea and he were very close friends. They shared similar life experiences, they were of the same generation. Both would enter the priesthood as young adults. My father chose Holy Cross and was posted for some time in Montreal. Neil was a Jesuit, and spent some time in Michigan. After the tumult of the 60s left its scar on the Catholic Church both men left the priesthood within two years of each other. This was certainly part of their bond, but their friendship ran deeper and wider than this, and it grew with them through the years. My father left the church in 1969 and I was born one dark December morn in 1970. When I was a mere three months old as I lay squirming with delight on my father's lap, rolling and kicking in the wide expanse of his corduroy, my mother grabbed the camera. My father was engrossed, however, in the book he was reading, a book a friend had given to him, and within minutes I drifted asleep, bored with no response.

This was the moment the picture was taken, and this photo, which I have guarded preciously since my adolescence, shows my father reading Neil McKenty's *Mitch Hepburn*. So, to me, Neil was the name on the book on my dad's bookshelf, and he was the name on the book in the photo. Those were the most real features, to me, of Neil McKenty. Sometimes I would mix up the names and refer to him either as Neil Hepburn or Mitch McKenty. My father died when I was 19, completely unprepared for the ravages of the real world, totally sheltered from the raw winds of life. I was utterly crushed. I was too young to have been a really interesting man to my father, and what I wish most desperately now, now that I am much older, is to be able to have one or two conversations with him. He was a brilliant and much loved man, but to me he was my goofy and embarrassing dad. And whenever I get heartsick now I shrink much further into myself to think that I was ever embarrassed by my dad. All I have of my father is his books and my fading memories. When I heard that Neil had died, a small part of me felt as if my father had died again. Then I decided to read that book from that infant photograph and I hoped that somehow, by reading it, I could feel closer to both my father and Neil.

I read *Mitch Hepburn*, and I encountered the mystical voice of Neil. The scholarship is stunning. He breathes life into the biography. His style is eloquent and his language is learned. Rare words such as "ukase" are bandied about nimbly and enviably. And while what may seem to some a dull subject, in Neil's hands the former Premier of Ontario leaps back to life in a merry twinkle. Mitch Hepburn sparkles, as Neil, an interested and passionate observer, narrates from the wings the unfolding tragedy of a brilliantly doomed man. It is humbling and inspiring, as all truly great writing should be. The craft of writing is hard, relentless and often banal work. In this respect it is a vocation. Anyone can write, but few write well. As I look back what I realize most strongly is the element of grace which is present. Grace, to me, is the leavening agent, the midwife to all the ideas. And as I age I cannot help but realize the association of a holy spirit with this agent of grace.

Hemingway's advice to Morley Callaghan was "a writer is like a priest. He has to have the same feeling about his work." Writing is a sacred act of translation, of the witness to the transubstantiation of idea to word, and it is the writer who helps us understand the timeless and constantly repeated action of creation.

Neil translated as both a priest and a writer. He was able to see the nature of reality from both viewpoints, from the world of Jesuits to the world of type, and he delivered to us a priceless, multifaceted legacy.

Neil (on the right) and his brother Stafford
with their Grandfather Shea, 1933.

Appendix
Earlier Years

Neil's first speech given when he was nine years old.

WHEN GRANDAD WAS A BOY

I don't see why the power has to go off just when we are listening to the last game of the world series. I was cross and crosser still when Granddad, who was sitting on the porch next to me, began to chuckle. "Well, when I was a boy," he commenced. All thoughts of baseball and even the most thrilling game of the World Series were forgotten, for I knew that when Granddad began that way I was sure to hear something more interesting. "In those days we did not have radios, and not even electricity," he went on, "We used candles instead and we had to make them at home."

"But Grandfather, how do you make candles? I thought you bought them from a store?"

"Well, the tallow was rendered from sheep and beef, poured into metal moulds, perhaps a dozen at a time and allowed to harden. My part of the work began then. Often when I came home from school, I helped mother undo the knots at the bottom of the moulds and pull them out from the top. There were no flashlights in those days either. We did the chores by the light of a home-made lantern in which one of those candles was placed. By the light of those flickering tallow candles we studied our lessons.

We didn't have the long summer holidays that you have now. At one time they were only one week, then two weeks, and later they were for three weeks. I spent mine at home helping with the crops."

"But Grandfather, you work all the time – didn't you have any fun?"

"Oh yes, but it was different from what you call fun. We used to sit around the fire in the evenings when someone told stories, most often ghost stories. There I would sit in the corner, listening and shivering, to creep off to bed as thirsty as I could be, because to run through that awful darkness from the house to the pump was more than I dared. We all looked forward to getting to the fall fair. It was one of the most important events of the year, and we certainly wasted no time in seeing that the potatoes were dug by the second week in October to make sure we could go. We often went to our neighbours to help with the work too, logging, threshing, husking, and woodcutting. The work went much faster when there were so many helping. Then there was time for fun when we finished.

In those days we did not use a binder, but cradled the wheat. One fall at our farm, five or six men cradled 50 acres. We had no time to bin the grain, but tied it with a band of the straw. When the grain was threshed we took it to some of the nearest towns, Peterboro, Colborne and Trenton. Once I had to take a load of 65 or 70 bushels of grain to market. There were five or six teams, travelling together and going to Brighton. We got up at two o'clock in the morning because it was a whole day's journey. We took along hay to feed the horses as it was such a long trip. The teams kept coming in from the whole countryside so that by nightfall there were 100 teams in Brighton. When I went back to look for my team I couldn't find them, there were so many horses in the barn. When we went to church in those days the whole family went in the wagon for there were no buggies. The first buggies were used around 1870. They were rather clumsy, and there weren't many of them.

"How far did you have to go, and how long did it take, Grandfather?" I asked.

"It was about two miles and it took a half an hour."

Surely a difference from the few seconds it took me to get to church in my dad's car, I thought.

"There were no milking machines or separators in those days either," he went on. "We had about 18 or 20 cows at home. The milk was put in earthen pans and set for the night. In the morning it was skimmed. We used dash churns to make the butter and it often took hours before any signs of butter appeared. Butter was packed in firkins, small wooden tubs made by coopers in the nearby village.

Washing the sheep in the spring was hard work too. They were sheared and the wool rolled in a sheet or a blanket, was pinned with thorns and taken to the carding mill in the village. After that was done the rolls were taken home and the wool was spun into yarn by the women of the household on the spinning wheel. It was now ready for the weaver, perhaps some local farmer, who had learned the art in the old country. Then the full cloth and flannels were taken home to be made into clothes. A tailor would go from house to house, sit on the table, and make the cuts. Every boy had a new full cloth suit, bound with black braid, to start off to school in the fall. And a new pair of boots, which were made by hand. We made our own sleighs too, out of the staves of barrels with pieces of boards to hold them together. We had just as much fun with them as you do now with a new toboggan.

One day at noon time, 15 or 20 boys went sleigh riding on the hill beside the school. I went too. It was far enough away so the teacher could not see us. We stayed there until 3 o'clock. We forgot all about school. School was let out, each one of us got four slaps with an oak ruler on our bare hand. Just as one of the boys went out the door, he – well – he said something that wasn't very nice to the teacher and away he went. The next day all the boys in the school were kept in after four to see how the boy would be punished. He was told to stand on the floor and take his coat off. He wouldn't do it, so it had to be taken off. He was slapped across the back with a blue beech rod with the frost taken out of it. He was given about 20 lashes. He didn't try any of those tricks again.

The making of maple sugar was both work and play. About 100 trees were tapped in our bush. The operations were all carried out in the woods. Wooden spiles, troughs, and yokes made by hand were used. The sap was carried in these to the boiling-down pots, big iron pots hung on a pole over the fire. Sugaring off took place about twice a week. It was fun for us when we were allowed to fill empty egg shells with the hot sugar and then eat it when it cooled."

"That would be fun Grandfather, I think you had as much fun when you were a boy as we do now, just different, that's all."

The door opened and dad walked in. "Well it was a great game," he said. I looked at him blankly. Could it be possible that the game was over while I was listening to Grandfather's story?

It was.

In 1951, when he was still a priest, Neil wrote *Holiday Memories*, which appeared in the *Jesuit Bulletin*.

The bay was clear and fresh in the bright morning sunshine. Here and there pools of light and shadow reflected the fluffy clouds hanging like tiny puffs of white smoke in the blue sky. And the dark spruce skyline, penciled with slender white poplars, was so sharp and close that it might have been painted on a coloured backdrop hung just behind the ridge.

Our tan cedar skiff slid easily through the water, her double oars flashing and dripping silver drops in the sunlight. There was no sound but the soothing swish of running waters and the sharp morning cry of birds, clear as an icicle.

No one spoke. The three Jesuit scholastics in the boat were making their morning meditation. For a Jesuit there is no holiday from this, ever, nor from morning Mass which we had just heard at our villa chapel overlooking lovely Lake Joseph. Somehow it is easy to pray here in this enchanted spot as the frosty mists roll up from the water and the sun's early rays fall on the tree tops about the hidden valley where the chapel is. No, it is not too difficult to think about God here, so prodigally strewn are his gifts of water and air and sky. To keep one's eyes clean and one's ears quiet, and one's mind serene, to breathe God's air, to work under His sky, that is the perfect holiday.

Meditation over, we slip quietly into the broad lake polished and gleaming like a silver paten. Over there snuggled behind two gashed rocks lies Angel's Cove. This is a delightful haunt for a sunny afternoon. One may swim in the clear water or read in the tracerwork of light under the spruce. There is a room on the flat rocks to set up an easel and sketch the wide expanse of water and rolling wooded hills. Back through the woods wind shady trails for hiking. Islands sprout up around us now. Bright yellow and white cottages, resembling doll houses in their setting of green shrubbery, peep out from behind the islets. Sleek motor launches skip about between the islets. Their gleaming prows tossing spray leap out of the water like greyhounds straining at a leash. We wave to one of the boats riding the swells nearby, its two occupants busy fishing. At the bottom of the lake a modern hotel, with stone turrets flung up above the pines, stands out in a sweep of smooth green lawns flowing down to the water's edge. Just as we row under a narrow bridge into Lake Rosseau, a yellow seaplane wheels out of the sun, skims down, and taxis sloppily across the water like a great wounded bird.

Around the spur of a rock we come upon a shady cove and stop for lunch. But first there is the fifteen minute examination of conscience, made walking under the trees over the soft fragrant pine needles. The Jesuits' spiritual exercises, lasting nearly three hours each day, are not cut down in holiday time. As a matter of fact, after ten months of intense study, his much needed three weeks rest is capped by an eight day retreat. For the past few years the annual retreat has been made at the summer house.

After a brisk swim and a delicious lunch we stretch out under the trees for a bit of a rest before starting the row home. Flies drone lazily in the sleepy sunshine while overhead the soft billowy clouds flap about in the fresh breeze.

Off again about four. Lake Rosseau's choppy surface is a patchwork of whitecaps. Soon we slip into the Joe River leading back to Lake Joseph. This is a picturesque stream set between ridges swaddled in spruce and pine. It curves through scarred rocks shattered to make a channel so narrow in spots that our oar-tips brush the shore. Sunlight glances off the quiet waters and so still is the deep afternoon that the boat might be moving across a painted landscape, flowing with greens and blues and suffused with golden light.

Back in Lake Joseph now, rowing into the sunset. The white wings of a gull poised motionless on a glistening rock are tinted pink in the flush of light. An air of mystery hovers over the water as the evening shadows deepen. The shore line falls back into the misty purple haze and over the darkness sounds the eerie wail of a loon.

As the boat glides silently into the dock we are just finishing the Rosary. At the top of the bluff one can see the last rays of the sinking sun flame up behind the ridge across the darkening bay. And through the chapel window the warm glow of the sanctuary lamp flickering before the Blessed Sacrament welcomes us home.

Regiopolis

After Neil died Catharine attended the multi-generational celebration of Regiopolis-Notre Dame High School's 175th anniversary in October 2012. Neil taught there in the early 1950s. The 1954 yearbook shows him surrounded by the keen members of the debating society, at ease in the book-lined, tall-shelved school library. There is Joe Coyle the president and Ed Koen, the vice-president, with their team who have just won a prize from radio station CKWS.

"I can still visualize Neil after all these years," Ed remembers. "He was a pretty commanding personality in the classroom. He taught us to articulate. There was no mumbling or slurring your words, no sloppy diction. I can still hear him pronouncing the word 'squirrel,' exaggerating each syllable until you could practically see the little critter scampering across the room. I was a bit introverted. Quite shy, having grown up on a farm 12 miles north of Kingston and gone to a one-room wooden schoolhouse. Imagine the impact of coming to Regi with its cosmopolitain student body from all over North, Central and South America, Mexico and China. Our football quarterback. Palyeo Gutierrez, was later shot with all his family during the Cuban revolution.

Neil understood where I was coming from and encouraged me, pushed me along. I can still remember the excitement of the debating society trip to Hastings, the small town where Neil had grown up. I think we stayed in the rectory.

Neil, right, with the program director of CKWS Kingston,
and the prize-winning debater.

There were some real characters among the students, wild-oats types sent by their harried parents to shape up. Jesuit discipline for those 40 years when they ran the school was pretty strict. Some of the wilder students considered it much like a penitentiary. Any noise after lights out in the dorm resulted in two hours on your knees out on the hard floor of that drafty corridor."

Neil taught us English and History. When I was still in Grade 12 he encouraged me and others to have a shot at preparing and trying for one of the tough Grade 13 exams, and he spent hours tutoring us to get us through. I also remember one day when he was briefly out of the classroom a fellow sitting near me got fed up with the mess of old notes in the wooden drawer of his school desk and set fire to them. The whole drawer went wildly up in flames, so he simply picked it up and calmly chucked it out the window – luckily there were no repercussions that time.

The Inside Story

It was my birthday, New Year's Eve 1994, about six months after my depression had lifted for good and the happiest summer of my life. Catharine and I had spent the afternoon cross-country skiing and were relaxed before supper in the lounge of the Laurentian Lodge Club at Prévost, amid the soft rolling foothills. Outside the frosted windows, the moonlight was glittering on the fresh snowfall; inside, a roaring fire flamed up the chimney of the large stone fireplace. A splendid dinner was prepared by our talented chef, André. I was presented with a birthday cake and a rousing chorus of three score years and ten. I don't remember feeling happier. I felt connected in a way I had never felt connected before to these people who were my friends. I laughed, and it was a genuine laugh. In some measure I had become real. I was comfortable in my skin. As I sat there in the dancing light of the fireplace and happy sounds of singing, I thought of all the people including my family and the Jesuits and my friends who had helped me on this journey. I thought of how God does indeed write straight with crooked lines. And then I thought, with Catharine smiling beside me, the best is yet to be.

From Neil's book, *The Inside Story*

"Catharine, Don't Panic"

In the end, no matter what, Neil could always make me laugh. I remember one particular December evening in our beloved farmhouse home in the heart of Victoria Village. On dark nights such as this one I always made sure to place candles of all sizes on an ancient dining room table which we bought for $35 from neighbours who were moving out as we were moving in. On this winter evening I had set a scrumptious shepherd's pie in front of Neil so he could serve us both. As he reached across the table to hand me my plateful the fuzzy sleeve of his bright red dressing gown caught fire.

To my horror the flames began to run up his arm. Neil quietly stood up, stepped out from the table, and moved steadily towards the kitchen saying calmly to me "Catharine, don't panic."

I followed him out to the kitchen, picked up a big green canister of flour from the counter and threw the contents over him. The fire went out. Neil returned to the meal as though nothing had happened, sitting there in his black-tinged dressing gown while I dissolved in near hysterical laughter.

Many times since, in moments of crisis, I hear those words, "Catharine, don't panic!"

They have often returned to stand me in good stead.

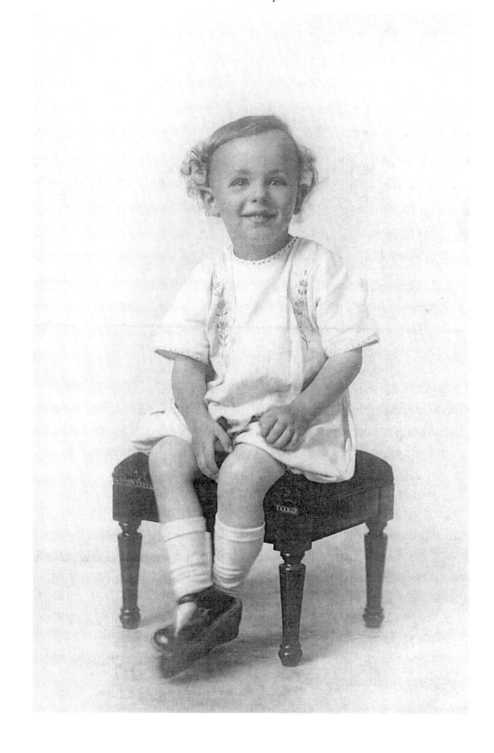

Chronology

1924
Dec. 31, Born in Peterborough, Ontario

1934
At Lady of Mount Carmel Catholic grade school, he is selected
to enter a local oratorical contest

1940–44
Newspaper stringer, *Toronto Star*, *Peterborough Examiner*

1938–1942
Campbellford High School

1942–43
Regiopolis College, Jesuit boarding school, Kingston

1943–44
St. Michael's College, University of Toronto

1944
Enters Society of Jesus novitiate, Guelph

1946–48
Juniorate, Guelph

1948
Philosophy, Jesuit Seminary, Toronto History, University of Toronto

1951
B.A. Philosophy, University of Montreal

1951–54
Senior teacher, History and English, Regiopolis College, Kingston

1955
Joins Jesuit order, four-year course in theology, Jesuit Seminary, Toronto

1954–56
Senior editor, *Jesuit Bulletin*

1956–59
Articles for *Globe and Mail*, CBC radio and television programmes including a series on Canadian books

1957
Ordained

1958
Assistant editor, (New York City, summer assignment) *America* (Jesuit current affairs weekly) Cleveland, tertianship

1959–60
Public relations and fund-raising for the new Jesuit seminary, Toronto

1960–61
Associate editor *The Way* (a new spiritual periodical) (London, England)

1963
M.A., Canadian History, University of Toronto

1965
M.A., University of Michigan, Communications: broadcast journalism, radio and TV writing, producing, directing

1965–67
Researches and writes biography, *Mitch Hepburn* (Premier of Ontario,1934–42). Published 1967. Toronto: McClelland and Stewart. Winner UBC Medal for Canadian Biography.

1969
Southdown Addiction Treatment Centre Decides to leave the priesthood.

1970–72
Executive Director, Foster Foundation for the Intellectually Handicapped (Toronto), Special Olympics

1972
Marries Catharine Fleming Turnbull, August 19; they move to Montreal.

1972–77
Begins new career at Radio Station CJAD as Public Affairs Director. Writes and broadcasts editorials, interviews, round tables. Assignments included Watergate hearings in Washington, D.C.; President Reagan press conference. He later co-hosted a 60-minute phone-in show with Hélène Gougeon.

1977–85
Solo two-hour morning talk show "Exchange"

1985
Leaves CJAD at the peak of his career (75,000 listeners) to finish John Main biography.

1986
In the Stillness Dancing: The Journey of John Main. Published by Darton, Longman & Todd, London; Crossroad, New York

1987–90
CFCF (Montreal) TV talk show host

1990
Leaves to focus on writing

1997
The Inside Story: Journey of a former Jesuit priest and talk show host towards self-discovery. Published by Shoreline Press, Montreal

2000
Skiing Legends and the Laurentian Lodge Club: A History of Skiing in the Laurentians, Catharine McKenty co-author. Published by Price-Patterson, Montreal.

Winner of the International Skiing History Association Skade Award, 2002, Vail, Colorado

2003
The Other Key: An Inspector Julian Main Mystery.

Published by Price-Patterson, Montreal

2008
Senior Times columnist; begins a blog

2012
May 12, McKenty dies at Montreal General Hospital, at the age of 87.

Board member of Nazareth House (a refuge for homeless men), Benedict Labre House (a centre for street people), Desta Black Youth Initiative.

Books by Neil McKenty

Mitch Hepburn

In the Stillness Dancing; The Journey of John Main

The Inside Story

The Other Key

Skiing Legends and the Laurentian Lodge Club, with Catharine McKenty.

See also: www.neilmckenty.com for more of Neil's columns, also radio and TV shows.

About the Editor

Veteran journalist Alan Hustak is the author of several books including *Faith Under Fire*, the biography of Frederick Scott, Canada's Extraordinary Chaplain of the Great War, *Sir William Hingston, 1829–1907, Montreal Mayor, Surgeon and Banker, Titanic, The Canadian Story*, and *At the Heart of St. Mary's*.

A recipient of the Queen's Diamond Jubilee medal, he divides his time between Montreal and Fort Qu'Appelle, Saskatchewan.